NEW JERSEY WILDLIFE VIEWING GUIDE

Laurie Pettigrew

D1372962

FALCON®

HELENA, MONTANA

Design, typesetting, and other prepress work by Falcon® Publishing,
Helena, Montana. Printed in Korea.

Defenders of Wildlife and its design are registered marks
of Defenders of Wildlife, Washington, D.C.
Watchable Wildlife® is a registered trademark of Falcon® Publishing.

Library of Congress Cataloging-in-Publication Data

Pettigrew, Laurie.
    The New Jersey wildlife viewing guide / by Laurie Pettigrew.
      p.   cm.
    Includes index.
    ISBN 1-56044-569-6 (pbk.)
    1. Wildlife viewing sites—New Jersey—Guidebooks. 2. Wildlife watching—
New Jersey—Guidebooks. 3. New Jersey—Guidebooks.
    I. Title.
    QL 193.P48   1998
    599.09749—DC21   97-6081
                                       CIP

Front cover photo: Pine Barrens tree frog
by Breck P. Kent

Back cover photo: Black bear cubs by Len Rue, Jr.

Author: Laurie Pettigrew
New Jersey Division of Fish, Game, and Wildlife

State Project Coordinator: James C. Sciascia
New Jersey Division of Fish, Game, and Wildlife

Diversity Tour Consultant: Mary Jeanne Packer

Wildlife Viewing Guide Program Manager:
Kate Davies, Defenders of Wildlife

Illustrator: Jane Eyre

CONTENTS

FUNDING SOURCES

N.J. Division of Fish, Game & Wildlife,
Endangered & Nongame Species Program

This guide was made possible, in large part, by funds raised from sales of New Jersey's Conserve Wildlife license plates. Additional funds were raised through the "Check-off for Wildlife" box on state income tax forms. Funds from both of these sources are used to preserve New Jersey's rich wildlife heritage and to provide additional opportunities for everyone to learn about and enjoy wildlife. Many of the sites in this guide will be improved with funding from federal grants and matching funds made available from Conserve Wildlife license plate revenue.

Conserve Wildlife plates are available at local Department of Motor Vehicles offices or by calling (609) 292-6500. At tax time, remember to help out New Jersey's wildlife by marking the "Check-off for Wildlife" box on your state income tax form. Your contribution goes a long way toward keeping New Jersey's wildlife wild.

PROJECT SPONSORS

 The New Jersey Department of Environmental Protection, DIVISION OF FISH, GAME AND WILDLIFE is a professional environmental organization dedicated to the protection, management, and wise use of the state's fish and wildlife resources. In addition to its statewide wildlife research and management activities, the division is responsible for 99 wildlife management areas encompassing 230,000 acres of diverse and productive habitats. These areas are funded with hunting and fishing license revenues and federal money collected from excise taxes on firearms, ammunition, and fishing tackle. Wildlife viewing improvements on the 18 Wildlife Management Areas featured in this guide were funded with New Jersey Green Acre Bond funds.

 DEFENDERS OF WILDLIFE is a national nonprofit organization of more than 200,000 members and supporters dedicated to preserving the natural abundance and diversity of wildlife and its habitat. A one-year membership is $20 and includes a subscription to *Defenders*, an award-winning conservation magazine. To join, or for further information, write or call Defenders of Wildlife, 1101 Fourteenth Street NW, Washington, DC 20005; (202) 682-9400. Visit their web site at http://www.defenders.org.

 The New Jersey Department of Commerce and Economic Development, DIVISION OF TRAVEL AND TOURISM is the government agency responsible for the marketing and development of the state as a leading travel destination. The division creates and administers a wide array of programs, services, and facilities to generate tourism revenues. Its overall mission is to increase tourism, contributing to the state's economic growth and quality of life. For more information, contact the NJ Division of Travel and Tourism, P.O. Box 826, Trenton,NJ 08625-0826; 1 (800) Jersey-7 or www.state.nj.us/travel.

&EPA The U.S. ENVIRONMENTAL PROTECTION AGENCY (EPA) is responsible for the administration of federal watershed management plans and nonpoint source control programs, federal water pollution control programs for municipal and industrial point sources, industrial pretreatment and storm water, toxic control programs, air pollution control programs, pollution prevention programs, and Superfund and other hazardous waste programs. EPA Region II is supporting New Jersey's Watchable Wildlife effort with funds from the Pollution Prevention Incentive for State's Grants Program.

 The U.S. FISH AND WILDLIFE SERVICE is pleased to support this project in furtherance of its mission to conserve, protect, and enhance fish and wildlife resources and their habitats. Additional funding for this project was provided through Partners for Wildlife, a federal aid grants program administered by the U.S. Fish and Wildlife Service. For further information, contact the U.S. Fish and Wildlife Service, 300 Westgate Center Drive, Hadley, MA 01035; 413-253-8200.

PSEG PUBLIC SERVICE ELECTRIC AND GAS COMPANY (PSE&G) is the largest power utility in New Jersey and the fourth-largest utility in the United States. PSE&G is committed to aggressive standards for corporate, economic, social, and environmental responsibility. PSE&G's Estuary Enhancement Program (EEP) is responsible for restoring and protecting more than 20,500 acres of salt marsh and adjacent uplands along the Delaware Estuary. PSE&G is pleased to be a supporter of the Watchable Wildlife program. For more information: PSE&G EEP, PO Box 236, M/C N33, Hancocks Bridge, NJ 08038; 1 (888) MARSHES.

 The DIVISION OF PARKS AND FORESTRY is dedicated to the stewardship of the state's rich and diverse historic, cultural, recreational, and natural resources for the benefit of present and future generations. The division manages and protects existing resources and identifies future needs while promoting a preservation and conservation ethic to perpetuate our natural and historic heritage. Twenty state parks and forests are listed as viewing sites in this guide.

 The DEPARTMENT OF DEFENSE is the steward of about 25 million acres of land in the United States, many of which contain irreplaceable natural and cultural resources. The DOD is pleased to support the National Watchable Wildlife Program through its Legacy Resource Management Program, a special initiative to enhance the conservation and restoration of natural and cultural resources on military land. For more information contact ODUSD (ES) EQ-LP, 3400 Defense Pentagon, Room 3E791, Arlington, VA 20301-3400.

 The NATIONAL PARK SERVICE is charged with administering the units of the National Park System in a manner that protects and conserves their natural and cultural resources for the enjoyment of present and future generations. For general information about units in New Jersey, contact the regional office: National Park Service, 200 Chestnut Street, Philadelphia, PA 19106; (215) 597-7018.

 The NEW JERSEY DEPARTMENT OF TRANSPORTATION manages 10,800 miles of the most intensely used transportation system in the nation. Because the quality of life of its citizens and visitors is one of its main goals, NJDOT is upgrading its signs, rehabilitating its roadsides and adding more sponsors for its successful Adopt A Highway litter and landscape programs. New Jersey maps and tourist information are available by calling 1-800-JERSEY7.

NEW JERSEY AUDUBON SOCIETY (NJAS) is a privately supported, not-for-profit, statewide membership organization. Founded in 1897, NJAS is independent of the National Audubon Society. NJAS operates eight nature centers and 26 sanctuaries; fosters environmental awareness and a conservation ethic among New Jersey residents; protects New Jersey's wildlife and plants, especially threatened and endangered species; and is committed to preservation of New Jersey's natural habitats. For more information contact New Jersey Audubon Society, 9 Hardscrabble Road, Post Office Box 126, Bernardsville, NJ 07924; (908) 204-8998; www.nj.com/audubon.

State of New Jersey

Department of Environmental Protection

New Jersey is blessed with a rich diversity of fish and wildlife. From the shores of Cape May Point to the mountains of Sussex County, more than 800 species of wildlife live in our state. One of my greatest pleasures as governor has been visiting the many wild and scenic places that can be found throughout New Jersey.

I am proud of the fact that we have set aside nearly 1 million acres of open space in an effort to preserve these places. Indeed, our state's fish and wildlife resources are extremely valuable not only for their recreational and aesthetic worth, but for the economic boost they give to the state's economy. Fishing, hunting, birding, feeding and photographing wildlife, and other outdoor activities contribute $2.65 billion in economic activity annually. In fact, thousands of small businesses, such as corner gas stations and local restaurants, profit from money spent by people enjoying wildlife-focused recreation.

For New Jerseyans and visitors alike, the Watchable Wildlife Program is a win-win situation. Everyone enjoys the vast outdoors while wildlife benefits from a heightened sense of public awareness and stewardship.

One of New Jersey's greatest assets is the richness and diversity of its fish and wildlife resources. I hope you will take the time to explore with this guide. I think you will be pleasantly surprised to discover the small wonders of our state.

Christine Todd Whitman
Governor

ACKNOWLEDGMENTS

This viewing guide was made possible by the New Jersey Division of Fish, Game and Wildlife's Endangered and Nongame Species Program, which provided both the impetus and major funding for the project. Support and contributions have come from numerous conservation groups and individuals. The *New Jersey Wildlife Viewing Guide* Steering Committee included: William E. Anderson of the NJ Department of Transportation; David Chanda of the NJ Division of Fish, Game and Wildlife; William Foelsch of the NJ Recreation and Parks Association; Frank Gallagher of the Division of Parks and Forestry; Anne Heasly of The Nature Conservancy; George P. Howard of the NJ Federation of Sportsmen's Clubs; William Neil of the NJ Audubon Society; Linda Rubenstein of the U.S. Fish and Wildlife Service; Jonathan C. Savage of the NJ Division of Travel and Tourism; and Janet C. Wolf of the National Park Service, NJ Coastal Heritage Trail. Their support and assistance with site nominations and text review was greatly appreciated.

The Division of Fish, Game, and Wildlife thanks all those whose special knowledge of the state's natural areas contributed to the guide. Nominations were submitted by numerous county parks and recreation departments, conservation organizations, wildlife biologists, park rangers, foresters, birdwatchers, and other individuals. Special thanks go to Dave Chanda, Frank Gallagher, Rich Hall, Anne Heasly, Diana Jones, Carol Nash, Kathy Porutski, Paul Tarlowe, and Ken Thompson, all of whom helped make the project manager's and author's job easier in many ways. The agency expresses gratitude for the calm support and encouragement we received from Kate Davies, Jane Eyre, and Scott Stepanski.

In addition, the New Jersey Division of Fish, Game, and Wildlife would like to acknowledge Karenne Snow, initial project manager, for her contributions to this guide. Karenne conducted the site visits and wrote many of the site descriptions.

INTRODUCTION

One of New Jersey's greatest assets is the richness and diversity of its wildlife, which is made possible by the variety of ecosystems and habitats found within the state. Whether used to describe the variety of wildlife found in the state or the regional Wildlife Diversity Tours themselves, diversity is what you will find as you explore New Jersey.

In this guide, New Jersey has been divided into eight physiographic regions, each with its own unique physical characteristics, shaped during New Jersey's fascinating geologic history. Over time, large-scale geologic events have created a 7,514-square-mile gem that has more to offer than other states many times its size.

Its diversity of habitat enables New Jersey to sustain more than 800 species of wildlife. Each spring, the state is host to the largest concentration of shorebirds in North America; and each fall, thousands of raptors, songbirds, bats, and butterflies pass through on their journeys south. New Jersey is also home to 41 endangered and 21 threatened wildlife species.

The purpose of this guide is to direct you to wildlife viewing sites across a broad spectrum of New Jersey's topography. Almost 120 sites were carefully evaluated using criteria developed by a steering committee made up of representatives from many fields, including: biologists, educators, conservationists, and transportation and tourism officials. The *New Jersey Wildlife Viewing Guide* describes 87 of these wildlife viewing sites, an assortment of locations where animals may be viewed in their natural surroundings. With the help of this viewing guide you will discover where and when to see New Jersey's wealth of wildlife.

As you enjoy New Jersey and its wild creatures, remember to act responsibly and appreciate the public lands and open spaces of this state. Please support the many agencies and private organizations that work to protect New Jersey's natural areas and open spaces. Together, we can ensure their existence for future generations.

WILDLIFE DIVERSITY TOURS

Wildlife Diversity Tours are a new addition to the Watchable Wildlife program, and are unique to the *New Jersey Wildlife Viewing Guide*. The written descriptions of the Wildlife Diversity Tour sites in the Ridge and Valley, Highlands, Cape May–Delaware Bay, and Pinelands regions are meant to provide in-depth information about each region as a whole, allowing wildlife viewers to gain a broader perspective as they string individual sites together into a tour.

These four regions are the least developed of the eight presented in this guide and have the greatest amount of open, public space. The purpose of the tours is to encourage multiday excursions to these regions, providing ecotourist-related economic development opportunities for communities that host large public land holdings.

An ideal way to experience a tour is to take a leisurely two-day trip, visiting each of the five tour sites in a region. Visiting all five tour sites in a region will provide an overview of the region's dominant ecosystems, wildlife habitats, and wildlife populations. It will also give the visitor a better understanding of the critical role that the maintenance of large, unfragmented ecosystems plays in preserving wildlife populations and diversity in New Jersey.

Each of the four tour regions has a rich local culture that can be sampled by seeking and visiting its various historical attractions. Recreational opportunities abound, as do wineries, farm markets, and shops where each area's unique natural bounty can be sampled. So take a tour, experience New Jersey's cornucopia of wilderness, and support local businesses and communities that are instrumental in preserving that wilderness for the future.

NATIONAL WATCHABLE WILDLIFE PROGRAM

Watching wildlife is the fastest growing form of outdoor recreation in the U.S. today. The National Watchable Wildlife Program is a response to this popular pastime. More than 2.2 million New Jerseyans watch, feed, or photograph wildlife each year, and more than half of this enthusiastic population travels to do so.

The Watchable Wildlife Program is a nationwide cooperative effort between federal and state agencies, businesses, and citizen's organizations, designed to get people actively involved in wildlife appreciation and conservation. Opportunities to view wildlife are made possible by a network of well-chosen wildlife viewing areas, uniformly marked with signs displaying the program's logo—white binoculars on a brown background. Each program site in a state is described in that state's wildlife viewing guide, which includes directions, facilities descriptions, and a list of the wildlife found at each site.

In the *New Jersey Wildlife Viewing Guide*, look for Wildlife Diversity Tour sites in four regions, which were developed to provide an overview of the major ecosystems and wildlife populations in each region.

This viewing guide and the development of Wildlife Diversity Tours are the first steps in an ongoing process. Many of the sites found in this guide are already developed for wildlife viewing, many more will be upgraded in the coming months and years, and additional sites will be added in the future. Look for the brown and white binoculars signs as you drive the highways and byways of New Jersey. Take the time to stop and enjoy some of New Jersey's natural treasures.

Dolphins are an increasingly common sight along the New Jersey coast. The aquatic antics of these attractive marine mammals please wildlife watchers from Cape Cod to Florida. HERB SEGARS

TIPS FOR OBSERVING WILDLIFE

Look in the right place . . . at the right time

A habitat is an area that ensures the right combination of food, water, cover, and space for an animal's survival. Knowing a little about the connection between animals and their habitats will help you know where to look for wildlife.

For instance, you are less likely to see or hear birds near the ground or in the trees on windy days because the movement of vegetation, leaves, and branches masks their movements and birds sing less when it is windy. However, during migration in spring and fall, if the wind is still, thousands of birds are likely to converge on one area.

Knowing when to look is important, too. During the warmer months, many animals are less active during the heat of the day. Aspiring wildlife watchers who wait for the cooler hours of dusk or dawn are more likely to see animals.

Extend your senses

Wildlife have keen senses that are much more developed than ours. To help overcome your sensory shortcomings, try using special equipment: binoculars, a spotting scope, or some type of sound-enhancing listening device.

Blend into the surroundings

Wild animals are sensitive to disturbances in their environment. Observing them takes practice and patience. Try a few of these tips to increase your chances of observing wildlife:

Winter is a good time to observe wildlife. Many species which are nocturnal during the warmer months can be seen foraging during daylight hours in the winter. LEN RUE, JR.

- Approach from downwind; this will keep your scent behind you.
- Move only when necessary; walk very slowly and quietly.
- Keep still; animals look for movement.
- Crouch down; a tall human figure stands out in a landscape.
- Wear a wide-brimmed hat; it will hide your eyes.
- Use a blind; your car, a canoe, or a commercial blind provides good cover.

Bring a field guide (or two)

Field guides are handy for anyone who wants to identify wildlife and learn about natural history. Field guides come in all shapes, sizes, and degrees of detail. Study the wildlife species you expect to see before your visit, paying close attention to their identifying characteristics. Look up wildlife in your guide while your impressions are still fresh. Learn to look carefully (you may be rewarded with only a glimpse).

Come prepared

Check your Wildlife Viewing Guide and note what facilities are available at each site you plan to visit. Current state and county road maps are useful planning tools. Remember to bring anything you may need to make your trip more successful and comfortable, i.e., insect repellent, sunscreen, water, etc.

Respect wildlife

While helping you to watch wildlife is the goal of this guide, it is important to remember to do so respectfully. Learn to watch for signs of animal distress or nervousness and retreat if you detect them. Never touch or attempt to touch a wild animal, especially a young one. Never place yourself between a wild animal and its young or its food. If you find yourself in this position, lower your eyes and back away slowly. Never disturb nesting wildlife.

Respect the site and the rights of others

Many people will be visiting the wildlife viewing sites listed in this guide. Please stay on designated trails and roads to avoid trampling vegetation, disturbing nesting or feeding birds and animals, and contributing to erosion. Move through an area quietly, so others may enjoy a peaceful outing. Try to

Great blue herons reside in both freshwater and saltwater marshes, where they can often be seen stalking a meal. They feed on small fishes, frogs, snakes, and aquatic invertebrates.
CLAY MYERS

13

leave a site better than you found it. Carry a litter bag and pick up any litter you find. Remember that, in some cases, you are the guest of a private land-owner. Please respect their privacy and show your appreciation for their generosity by acting responsibly.

HOW TO USE THIS GUIDE

Your wildlife viewing guide contains a wealth of information. Please take a few moments to become familiar with its contents and organization.

This guide is divided into eight sections, representing the major physiographic regions of New Jersey. Each section opens with a full-color map that identifies the wildlife viewing sites within a region, a list of the major roads and towns in the area, and a detailed description of the region's dominant ecosystem. In four of these sections, you will find Wildlife Diversity Tours (see the Wildlife Diversity Tour section of the introduction).

The text for each viewing site includes a description of the area and wildlife viewing information. The site description section provides a brief overview of the various habitats at each site, followed by a viewing information section, which includes the probability of seeing selected species and the optimal months or seasons for viewing. Specific viewing locales within site boundaries are offered when possible. NOTES OF CAUTION RELATING TO ROAD CONDITIONS, SAFETY ISSUES, AREA CLOSURES, AND OTHER RESTRICTIONS APPEAR IN CAPITAL LETTERS.

Explicit directions are supplied for each viewing site. The name of the town closest to the site appears beneath the directions; in most cases, this is the nearest town offering fuel and a pay phone. In all cases, viewers should supplement the directions in this guide with an up-to-date state map, road atlas, county road map, or, in some cases, a topographic map. Viewing sites are marked with Wildlife Viewing Area signs displaying the brown-and-white binoculars logo.

The name and phone number of each site's managing agency, organization, or corporation is included with its description; feel free to contact them for more information. If there are several owners, more than one number may be present.

Recreational icons (identified below) appear at the bottom of each site account. These icons provide important information about recreational opportunities, parking, entrance fees, and restrooms.

FACILITY AND RECREATION ICONS

| Entry or Use Fee | Parking | Restrooms | Barrier-Free | Restaurant | Picnic Area | Lodging | Camping |

| Hiking | Bicycling | Cross-Country Skiing | Horse Trails | Boat Ramp | Large Boats | Small Boats |

14

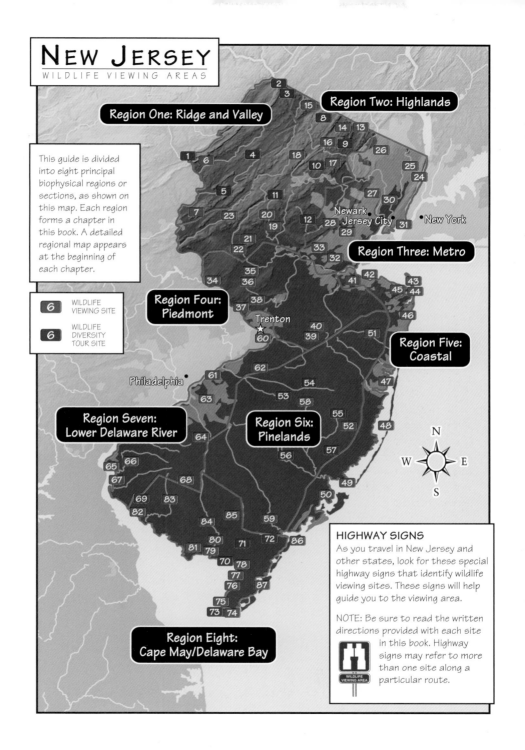

NEW JERSEY
WILDLIFE VIEWING AREAS

Region One: Ridge and Valley

Region Two: Highlands

This guide is divided into eight principal biophysical regions or sections, as shown on this map. Each region forms a chapter in this book. A detailed regional map appears at the beginning of each chapter.

6 WILDLIFE VIEWING SITE

6 WILDLIFE DIVERSITY TOUR SITE

Newark
Jersey City
New York

Region Three: Metro

Region Four: Piedmont

Trenton

Region Five: Coastal

Philadelphia

Region Seven: Lower Delaware River

Region Six: Pinelands

N
W   E
S

Region Eight: Cape May/Delaware Bay

HIGHWAY SIGNS

As you travel in New Jersey and other states, look for these special highway signs that identify wildlife viewing sites. These signs will help guide you to the viewing area.

NOTE: Be sure to read the written directions provided with each site in this book. Highway signs may refer to more than one site along a particular route.

WILDLIFE VIEWING AREA

One: Ridge and Valley

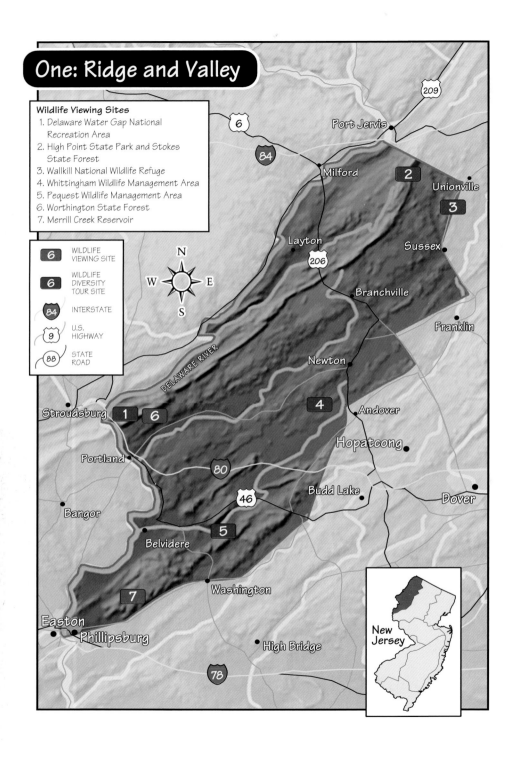

Wildlife Viewing Sites

1. Delaware Water Gap National Recreation Area
2. High Point State Park and Stokes State Forest
3. Wallkill National Wildlife Refuge
4. Whittingham Wildlife Management Area
5. Pequest Wildlife Management Area
6. Worthington State Forest
7. Merrill Creek Reservoir

6	WILDLIFE VIEWING SITE
6	WILDLIFE DIVERSITY TOUR SITE
84	INTERSTATE
9	U.S. HIGHWAY
88	STATE ROAD

N W E S

DELAWARE RIVER

209

6

84

Port Jervis

Milford

2

Unionville

3

Layton

206

Sussex

Branchville

Franklin

Newton

Stroudsburg   1   6

Andover

Hopatcong

Portland

80

Budd Lake

Dover

46

Bangor

5

Belvidere

Washington

7

Easton

Phillipsburg

High Bridge

78

New Jersey

RIDGE AND VALLEY

The Ridge and Valley Region is dominated by the Kittatinny Ridge, which runs northeast to southwest along the Delaware River. East of the ridge is a broad valley carved by a glacier estimated to have been a mile thick, during the last ice age. The soils of the ridge are typically shallow, rocky, and of poor quality, while the valley contains fertile soil and has a long history of agricultural activity.

The Appalachian Trail runs along the crest of the ridge and extends north to Maine and south to Georgia. The trail is accessible from many road crossings and numerous hiking trails.

The ridge itself runs north into New York and south into Pennsylvania. Its vegetation is characteristically oak-hickory and oak-maple forests on its flanks, with pitch pine–scrub oak communities along the summit. There are numerous hemlock ravines along the many brooks that flow off the ridge. The area's stands of pine and spruce date back to the New Deal conservation projects of the 1930s. Wetlands, large forested patches, and limestone fens are also prevalent on the ridge. Other notable features include the Delaware Water Gap, at the southern end of the ridge, and High Point State Park in the northwest corner of the state. Sunrise Mountain, in Stokes State Forest, is popular for its vistas and as a gathering place for viewing the annual migration of raptors in the fall. The ridge-and-valley topography creates air-flow patterns that aid a great number of raptors and other birds during migration.

Above: *One of the many vistas hikers can enjoy while trekking through the Delaware Water Gap National Recreation Area on the Appalachian Trail.*
LEN RUE, JR.

17

The area is rich in history as well as wildlife. The Old Mine Road, running along the Delaware from the Water Gap to Port Jervis, New York, is the oldest commercial road in the U.S., and was originally constructed by the Dutch to transport copper from local mines, which are visible from a marked hiking trail. There are also countless old stone "fences" throughout the area, old cemeteries, and the historic villages of Walpack, Millbrook, and Peter's Valley.

Fortunately, much of the region, including the Kittatinny Ridge, is preserved as public land. The entire region is bordered on the west by the Delaware River, which supports a great diversity of fish and wildlife, including osprey, eagles, beavers, otters, and a variety of nesting waterfowl. The forested ridge gives birth to trout streams and fertile valleys, which provide a diversity of habitat for coyotes, bobcats, black bears, white-tailed deer, wild turkeys, and hundreds of hawks, owls, and songbirds. The agricultural areas of the Great Valley on the eastern side of the region, and the farmlands to the south, contribute to the diversity of the region.

Above: *Black bears are a common sight in northwestern New Jersey, especially in the mixed oak-hickory communities, wooded ridges, and rhododendron swamps of the Kittatinny Ridge.* LEN RUE, JR.

Opposite: *The Delaware Water Gap National Recreation Area preserves 70,000 acres in New Jersey and Pennsylvania, offering beautiful vistas and the opportunity to see an amazing diversity of wildlife.* DWIGHT HISCANO

MOUNTAIN LAUREL

RUFFED GROUSE

BRACKEN FERN

RED-TAILED HAWK

GLACIAL LAKE

PIKE

BROOK TROUT

WILD TURKEY

The ridges and valleys of this region are a result of differences in their parent rock. Soft limestone and shale erode faster than the more resistant conglomerates and sandstone, creating ridges and valleys. These differences affect the types of plants and animals that live here.

Mixed-oak forests dominate the ridges and provide abundant food for wildlife. White-tailed deer, black bears, wild turkeys, and ruffed grouse are a few of the species that feed on the ridges' abundant acorns, beech nuts, hickory nuts, wild grapes,

BLACKBURNIAN WARBLER

MAY APPLE

GREAT HORNED OWL

BLACK BEAR

BOBCAT

TROUT STREAM

COPPERHEAD

MINK

and blueberries. *Migratory neotropical birds thrive in these upland forests, feasting on insects and berries.*

Many rivers and streams flow through the limestone valleys, providing ideal water conditions for brook trout, New Jersey's only native trout. Glacial lakes provide a home for larger game fish, including northern pike.

Northern copperheads and timber rattlesnakes, New Jersey's only venomous snakes, seek out rocky outcroppings for temporary shelter and winter den sites.

1. DELAWARE WATER GAP NATIONAL RECREATION AREA

Description: The Delaware Water Gap is an amazing geological formation—a large break in the Kittatinny Ridge through which the Delaware River flows. The recreation area stretches along the northern reaches of the Delaware River for 37 miles, in both New Jersey and Pennsylvania.

The Appalachian Trail borders the eastern edge of the recreation area for half of its length, but there are a variety of other hiking and cross-country skiing trails as well. Visitors are likely to see white-tailed deer, porcupines, river otters, or perhaps even black bears, from the area's many trails.

Diversity Tour Information: The Delaware Water Gap National Recreation Area's Kittatiny Point Visitor Center is nestled in the gap, on the bank of the Delaware River. Stop in to get a map and current information about conditions and viewing opportunities in the park. The Delaware River Valley and the Delaware Water Gap have been important travel corridors, for both people and animals, for hundreds of years.

Each spring and fall, thousands of waterfowl migrate through the valley. The Poxono Boat Launch and the Copper Mine Trailhead parking areas are good places to go to watch the birds' seasonal movements. The launch area offers a great view of the river and Poxono Island, where bald eagles roost in winter and osprey are seen from April through September. The area is popular with eagles because they are able to find open water on the river year-round. These fish-eating birds have made a dramatic recovery in the gap in the past 25 years, thanks to regulations limiting industrial discharge into the river. The resultant improvement in water quality has bolstered fish populations,

providing more food for eagles and other wildlife. The river and its tributaries also provide food and habitat for river otters, common mergansers, and common goldeneyes.

The forested ridges on your right, as you continue north through historic Millbrook Village, are critical habitat for New Jersey's growing black bear and bobcat populations. These mammals hunt and live in the ridges' large tracts of undisturbed forest, which give them cover as they travel between areas. The forest is also the summer home for timber rattlesnakes when they leave their winter den sites in the rocky outcrops along Kittatinny Ridge. White-tailed deer, wild turkeys, and black bears are sometimes seen from the roads and trails, feeding on acorns and hickory nuts from the trees of this mixed-oak forest. Scattered clearings provide good feeding areas while the forest provides cover. During winter, scan the stands of evergreens for evening grosbeaks, purple finches, pine grosbeaks, and common redpolls. Late May to early July is the best time to see nesting pileated woodpeckers, cliff swallows, golden-crowned kinglets, solitary vireos, and blackburnian warblers.

Just over the ridge from Millbrook Village is the sparkling Flatbrook River, one of New Jersey's premier trout streams. Its crystal-clear water supports the delicate web of aquatic life that trout depend on for food. The water quality is so high because thousands of acres of forest and wetlands act as pollution filters and sediment traps.

From the Flatbrook, take Old Mine Road back toward Millbrook and take the first left (on unmarked Blue Mountain Lake Road), which will take you to Blue Mountain Lake. A short hike from the parking area takes you to the clear waters of this glacial lake (one of several in the area). Glacial lakes were created thousands of years ago, when glaciers scoured and gouged the ridgetops.

Continue past Blue Mountain Lake and Long Pine Pond to Skyline Drive, which leads to Crater Lake. Several pull-offs along this road give you breathtaking vistas of the forest, ponds, and wetlands in the valley below. These natural communities weave together into a complex that supports hundreds of wildlife spe-

Wood turtles depend on streams with good water quality: they breed in streams in the fall and hibernate in them in the winter. In the summer, they utilize a variety of wetland and upland habitats. BRECK P. KENT

cies. Several of the state's endangered animals rely on this unfragmented ecosystem for their survival—barred owls, red-shouldered hawks, Cooper's hawks, timber rattlesnakes, and bobcats, to name a few. These ridgetop

Opposite: *Van Campens Brook, a designated wild trout stream, hosts a population of native brook trout.* BRIAN P. BOWER

overlooks also provide excellent opportunities for viewing the fall hawk migration; look for sharp-shinned, broad-winged, and red-shouldered hawks.

As you leave this site, drive north through the recreation area along the Delaware River. The Old Mine Road is one of the oldest roads in the region, used by Dutch copper miners in the 17th century. Today, it is one of the most beautiful drives in the state, with the nationally designated Scenic Delaware River on one side and the Kittatinny Ridge on the other.

Directions: *Traveling west on Interstate 80, take exit 1 (last exit in New Jersey), the Old Mine Road exit. Turn left at the bottom of the exit ramp and follow the road to Kittatinny Point Visitor Center.*

Wildlife Diversity Tour Directions:

FROM DELAWARE WATERGAP NATIONAL RECREATION AREA (SITE 1)
TO HIGH POINT STATE PARK (SITE 2)

Leaving Millbrook Village in the DWNRA, take Millbrook Road north to County Route 615. Staying on CR 615, take the time to stop at Tillman Ravine Natural Area, Walpack Center, and Peters Valley. At the intersection of CR 615 and County Route 560, turn right (east) on CR 560. Follow CR 560 to its intersection with U.S. Highway 206. Turn right (south) and drive approximately 3 miles to Sunrise Mountain Road. Turn left and travel on Sunrise Mountain Road for approximately 9 miles. At this point, the road's name becomes Crigger Road. Continue on Crigger Road to its intersection with Deckertown Turnpike. Turn right and follow Deckertown Turnpike to its end at New Jersey 23. Turn left (north) on NJ 23 and proceed about 3 miles to the High Point State Park office on the left.

Ownership: National Park Service (973) 948-6500, (717) 588-2435

Size: More than 70,000 acres   **Closest Town:** Columbia

The timber rattlesnake, one of New Jersey's most endangered species, is timid and secretive. Females reach sexual maturity at 9 or 10 years of age and bear young only once or twice in their lifetime. BRECK P. KENT

24

2. HIGH POINT STATE PARK AND STOKES STATE FOREST

Description: New Jersey's highest point, at 1,803 feet, provides scenic vistas of the Kittatinny Ridge, Pennsylvania, and New York. High Point State Park borders the Delaware River Valley to the east, making it a good vantage point for hawk viewing during the fall migration. High Point habitats include upland forest, glacial lakes, streams, hardwood swamps, and ridgetop communities of endangered plant species.

Diversity Tour Information: The many wetlands in High Point State Park and the adjacent Stokes State Forest are home to beavers, otters, and great blue herons. These areas are an excellent example of the work of the industrious beaver, the creature directly responsible for creating and expanding the freshwater wetlands of northern New Jersey. What glacial activity began, the beaver has perpetuated with its ability to construct elaborate dams, lodges, and bank dens, which, along with the beaver's propensity for storing food for winter retrieval, makes it one of the few animals capable of modifying its habitat to meet its needs. Walk along the many streams in the valleys to see the impact that beavers have had on the local vegetation.

Both active dams and abandoned beaver meadows occur along the Big Flatbrook, between Deckertown Turnpike and Sawmill Lake in High Point State Park. Look for dams along Sawmill Road, which runs parallel to the stream. Also, look for two distinct zones of vegetation—the wetter sites are more densely covered by shrub thickets made up of alders, willow, and button bush; less-wet sites are forested with red maple and yellow birch. Both of these types of vegetation are a favorite food source for beavers. Beaver-created wetlands are frequented by many wildlife species, including muskrats, otters, and raccoons. Mallards, wood ducks, and black ducks also thrive in these small freshwater wetlands, as do many reptiles and amphibians.

The beaver, North America's largest rodent, fells hardwood trees by gnawing away at the trunk with their massive front teeth. When the tree falls, they eat the tender bark from the smaller branches and use the larger branches to build dams and lodges.
CHARLES H. WILLEY

Take Sunrise Mountain Road to enjoy the remarkable scenery of New Jersey's ridge country, complete with views into the neighboring state of Pennsylvania. The pavilion at Sunrise Mountain is barrier-free and a great spot to watch migrating hawks in the spring and fall.

Also look for rattlesnakes basking in the sun on the rocky outcrops of Sunrise Mountain. This region is one of only a few small areas where the timber rattlesnake is still found in New Jersey. Northern New Jersey's limestone rock outcroppings provide ideal denning sites. Rattlers tend to return to the same den sites year after year. Overcollecting and indiscriminate killing have reduced the timber rattlesnake to endangered species status in New Jersey.

The 850-acre Dryden Kuser Natural Area in the northern section of the park includes a distinctive cedar swamp and bog. It is the northernmost bog in New Jersey and contains many plants that are more typical of New England

than New Jersey. There is a 1.5-mile loop trail around the bog from which you can view the more than 30 species of birds that make the cedar swamp their home. More than 100 species pass through the swamp throughout the year. The abundant food supplied by the upland vegetation (many species of oaks, black huckleberry, and lowbush blueberry) attracts many species of wildlife, including white-tailed deer, black bears, porcupines, red foxes, and other smaller mammals. Listen for the pecking of a woodpecker or the drumming of a grouse.

Tillman Ravine Natural Area, in Stokes State Forest, offers visitors another easy, enjoyable walking tour. Tillman Ravine borders Brink Road, which runs from Wallpack Center through Stokes State Forest to Route 206. Begin the 0.5-mile loop trail from either of the two parking areas along the road marked Tillman Falls Scenic Area. The trail wanders through a hemlock-mixed hardwood forest, over the Tillman Brook, and into an oak–maple forest. The hemlock ravines are important travel corridors for black bears and bobcats, and provide nesting and feeding habitat for forest-dwelling raptors, including barred owls and goshawks.

In Stokes State Forest, some of the trees are over 100 feet tall, almost 4 feet in diameter, and thought to be over 150 years old. Large clumps of rhododendron and mountain laurel, witch hazel, or highbush blueberry provide food and cover for black bears. Unfortunately, many of the hemlock-mixed hardwood forests of New Jersey are now infested with an introduced Asiatic insect, the hemlock woolly adelgid. This aphidlike insect sucks juices from the needles of trees, causing them to lose vigor and die. Some areas of hemlock forest have already been killed and others are likely to follow.

Directions: *High Point State Park: From New Jersey 23 in Sussex Borough, follow NJ 23 north for 7 miles. The park office will be on the left (visible from the highway). Entrance to the park's day use area is on the right. Stokes State Forest: From New Jersey 206 in Branchville Township, follow NJ 206 north for 4 miles to the state forest office on the right.*

Wildlife Diversity Tour Directions:
FROM HIGH POINT STATE PARK (SITE 2)
TO WALLKILL NATIONAL WILDLIFE REFUGE (SITE 3)

From the High Point State Park office, take New Jersey 23 south for approximately 9 miles to County Route 565. Turn left and follow CR 565 1.4 miles to the refuge office on the left.

Ownership: NJDEP Division of Parks and Forestry. High Point State Park (973) 875-4800; Stokes State Forest (973) 948-3820

Size: High Point State Park: 14,192 acres, Stokes State Forest: 15,743 acres

Closest Towns: Colesville and Branchville

Opposite: *In spring, the delicate pinkish white blooms of mountain laurel dot slopes and ridgetops throughout High Point State Park and Stokes State Forest.*
DWIGHT HISCANO

3. WALLKILL NATIONAL WILDLIFE REFUGE

Description: The Wallkill River bottomland is one of the few large areas of high-quality waterfowl habitat remaining in northwestern New Jersey. The refuge provides critical habitat for American black ducks, mallards, green-winged teal, wood ducks, and Canada geese. The refuge straddles two major migration corridors for waterfowl that stop to rest and feed along the wetlands of the Wallkill River. Raptors and songbirds are plentiful during spring and fall migration.

Diversity Tour Information: Established in 1990, Wallkill National Wildlife Refuge is located along a 9-mile stretch of the Wallkill River. The Wallkill River lies within the Great Valley, which is bordered by the Kittatinny Mountain Range on the west and the Highlands Mountain ridges to the east. Because of these features, many migratory birds are "funneled" through the Wallkill Valley. More than 225 species of bird occur on the refuge, including 21 species of waterfowl, 32 species of waterbirds, 24 species of raptors, and 125 species of songbirds. The most common mammals are eastern cottontails, gray squirrels, raccoons, beavers, muskrats, red and gray foxes, eastern coyotes, and white-tailed deer. Occasionally, black bears and bobcats are observed passing through the valley.

The most outstanding feature of the Wallkill Valley is its broad and extensive floodplain. Early Dutch settlers dubbed the Wallkill River bottomland "The Drowned Lands," because the valley flooded extensively, forming a huge lake in the spring. Before they were effectively drained, settlers used the bottomland meadows as pasture for cattle. As early as 1760, efforts were made to straighten, dredge, and drain the river corridor to make the land dry enough to farm. The effort did not succeed until 66 years later, when a large canal lowered the water table of the river. Eventually, most, if not all, of the floodplain wetlands were drained. Over time, the river has begun to reclaim its floodplain wetlands. The refuge is being managed to help that process along and to preserve, restore, and enhance the natural diversity of fish, wildlife, plants, and their habitats along the Wallkill River.

A wildlife observation platform provides an overlook of a 300-acre area that is being restored by the refuge to provide habitat for migratory waterfowl and shorebirds. Before the refuge acquired this site, it was drained by a series of ditches and maintained as a sod farm. Through construction of a series of levees, channels, and water control structures, the once biologically sterile area now provides habitat for thousands of waterfowl and shorebirds, which are funneled through the Wallkill Valley each year during migration. Management of this site will provide a variety of moist soil habitats ranging from deeper pools for resting and feeding waterfowl and wading birds to mudflats for migrating shorebirds.

The Wood Duck Trail, a former railroad bed, is a good example of the natural wetland reclamation and restoration that is occurring on the broad Wallkill River floodplain. This 2.25-mile trail traverses a wetland community that includes a mix of wetland forest, wet meadow, and emergent wetlands on its path to the Wallkill River. Wetland reclamation has been sped along here by beaver activity, evidenced by the dams and beaver lodges along the trail.

The deeper water caused by beaver activity attracts muskrats, great blue herons, wood ducks, mallards, black ducks, and geese. The wet meadows and shrubs are good places to find woodcocks, phoebes, bluebirds, turkeys, and deer. The forested wetlands provide habitat for a wide assortment of nesting songbirds and warbler species during migration.

The hundreds of acres of upland grasslands and forests are important habitat for a variety of raptors and songbirds. The refuge plans to actively manage its many acres of grassland habitat for rare grassland bird species, including threatened grasshopper sparrows, savannah sparrows, endangered vesper sparrows, and upland sandpipers. Grassland habitat for these species is being lost at an alarming rate in New Jersey and throughout the northeast. Long-term management that will maintain large, contiguous blocks of short to medium-height grasses will be critical to these species as development and natural succession claim an increasing amount of grassland bird habitat.

As this new refuge acquires land, existing and permitted recreational activities, sites, and wildlife observation trails may change. Information on open areas, activities, and directions are available by visiting or calling the refuge office.

Directions: *From Sussex Borough, take New Jersey 23 south for 2 miles. Turn left onto County Route 565 north (CR 565 joins NJ 23 for 1 mile before turning north) and travel 1.4 miles to the refuge office, which is on the left.*

Wildlife Diversity Tour Directions:
FROM WALLKILL NATIONAL WILDLIFE REFUGE (SITE 3)
TO WHITTINGHAM WILDLIFE MANAGEMENT AREA (SITE 4)

From Wallkill NWR, take New Jersey 23 south to New Jersey 94. Turn right (west) on NJ 94 and proceed to U.S. Highway 206. Take US 206 south to County Route 618. Turn right and proceed 0.5 mile to Springdale Road. Turn left and continue 0.2 mile to the parking area for Whittingham WMA Big Springs Wetlands on the left.

Ownership: U.S. Fish and Wildlife Service (973) 702-7266

Size: Nearly 7,500 acres   **Closest Towns:** Sussex, NJ, and Unionville, NY

New Jersey has 600,000 acres of freshwater wetlands, which provide critical habitat for migratory birds such as this green-winged teal.
TOM VEZO

4. WHITTINGHAM WILDLIFE MANAGEMENT AREA

Description: Whittingham's extensive freshwater marsh and diverse upland forests and fields are home to a variety of wildlife. This wetland complex is the headwaters of the Pequest River. Numerous springs originate deep within the limestone bedrock. The springs' calcium-rich water bubbles to the surface and sustains the wetlands.

Diversity Tour Information: This site is divided into two distinct viewing areas. One is the freshwater marsh and wetlands visible from the parking area off of County Route 611. The other is the limestone-rich upland forest, accessible from the Springdale Road parking area. Plan to make a day of it here, to see all that this marvelous site has to offer. Spring and fall are the best viewing seasons, but summer and winter are loaded with wildlife viewing opportunities as well.

Freshwater marshes and wetlands like the headwaters of the Pequest were, until recently, considered wastelands, since they are too wet for most agricultural uses and not suitable for building lots. In many other places in New Jersey, these important ecosystems have been drained or filled. Fortunately, that was not allowed to happen here and today this wonderful natural area remains intact for wildlife and visitors alike to enjoy. Walk along the edge of the marsh to look for beavers, river otters, and other wetlands wildlife. Many species of waterfowl are present in different seasons, including nesting wood ducks, American black ducks, and mallards. Several different species of turtle reside in the freshwater marsh as well, including snapping, wood, and eastern painted turtles.

Whittingham Wildlife Management Area, in its fertile limestone valley, is one of northern New Jersey's most pristine upland forests. Because the soils were so rich, early settlers cleared these areas first and farmed them for many years. Today, much of the wildlife management area is naturally revegetating to a sugar maple–mixed hardwood forest ecosystem. While exploring the for-

Water flowing through underground limestone is rich in calcium, giving rise to limestone fens, which support rare plants and animals like this endangered bog turtle. Spring-fed wetlands, like the headwaters of the Pequest River, provide critical nesting habitat for bog turtles.
ROBERT T. ZAPPALORTI

ests, you may encounter the ruffed grouse (best known for its explosive flushes when approached too closely). Listen for the reverberating drumming sound males produce to attract mates in the spring.

In other parts of the area, wildlife biologists are maintaining the old farm fields, hedgerows, and brushlots for the important wildlife habitats they provide. In addition, area farmers lease some of the land to plant crops, but are required to leave a percentage of their crops to provide food for wildlife.

Many kinds of wildflowers flourish here because of the limestone rock and calcium-rich soil. In the spring, look for May apples, several species of violet, wood anemone, Solomon's-seal, jack-in-the-pulpit, wild sarsaparilla, Canada mayflower, and garlic mustard. In the summer and fall, you should be able to spy woodland asters, goldenrod, grasses, and ferns. The limestone is also home to many species of amphibian (wood frogs, spring peepers, American toads, and spotted salamanders) that live and breed in ephemeral pools in the forest. These small pools, and the larger marshes nearby, play an important role in maintaining water quality by absorbing excess nutrients and trapping and filtering sediments. They also act as temporary reservoirs for snowmelt and springtime floodwaters, reducing water turbidity and maintaining a more constant water-level downstream, to the benefit of both humans and wildlife.

The limestone deposits found here are all the evidence that is left of a great inland ocean that once covered much of the eastern seaboard. When this ancient sea drained, the ocean floor was layered with the shells and skeletons of the many aquatic creatures left behind by the receding waters. Their remains were compacted to form the limestone bedrock, bluffs, and other outcrops that you see here and at other sites in north Jersey.

The Whittingham Wildlife Management Area is a natural area with no facilities. OPEN FOR HUNTING DURING PRESCRIBED SEASONS.

Directions: *From the junction of U.S. Highway 206 and County Route 611, take CR 611 west for approximately 1 mile, to the wetland overlook on the right. From the overlook, go back to US 206 and turn left. Take the next left onto County Route 618. Proceed 1.4 miles and turn left onto Springdale Road. Proceed 0.2 mile to the parking area on the left. The trail from the parking area goes through the natural area to Big Spring wetlands.*

Wildlife Diversity Tour Directions:
FROM WHITTINGHAM WILDLIFE MANAGEMENT AREA (SITE 4)
TO PEQUEST WILDLIFE MANAGEMENT AREA (SITE 5)

From Whittingham WMA, take U.S. Highway 206 south 4–5 miles to County Route 517. Turn right on CR 517 and proceed approximately 12 miles into Hackettstown. Turn right onto New Jersey 46 west and travel 8 miles to the Pequest WMA entrance on the left.

Ownership: NJDEP, Division of Fish, Game, and Wildlife (908) 637-4125

Size: 1,753 acres   **Closest Towns:** Newton and Andover

5. PEQUEST WILDLIFE MANAGEMENT AREA

Description: The variety of habitats found at the Pequest Wildlife Management Area, including manmade ponds, natural rivers, fields, and upland forests, support many species of wildlife. The Pequest Trout Hatchery raises brook, brown, and rainbow trout. Self-guided hatchery tours are available at the Natural Resource Education Center, which also has interactive exhibits about the trout, state wildlife, and local geology. The center is open daily from 10 A.M. to 4 P.M. (closed holidays). Hiking trails through fields and upland forests start from the center picnic area.

Diversity Tour Information: The Pequest Trout Hatchery was built at this location because of its abundance of high-quality water. Completed in 1982, the state-of-the-art facility is designed to keep trout-production costs as low as possible and to prevent transmission of disease. Since 1984, the hatchery has produced more than 600,000 brook, brown, and rainbow trout each year, for stocking in 200 lakes and streams open to public fishing. A network of six wells at the hatchery, dug into one of the east coast's largest aquifers, supplies up to 7,000 gallons of water per minute. Special aerators maintain the high oxygen levels that the growing fish need to flourish. Automated feeding, transfer trucks, and controlled visitor access keep direct human contact with the fish to a minimum. Spring and fall are the most active seasons at the trout hatchery.

The Natural Resource Education Center contains a wealth of information about New Jersey's wildlife species. Interpretive programs are available throughout the year. Adjacent to the center, visitors can see a good demonstration of backyard wildlife habitat improvement and the Pequest Butterfly Garden. The garden is active from spring until fall. This is a good place to get some useful ideas to try at home. In just a small space, these areas provide habitat for a variety of butterflies, moths, hummingbirds, bluebirds, tree swallows, songbirds, and honey bees.

The Pequest Trout Hatchery raises over 600,000 brook, brown, and rainbow trout annually for release into more than 200 New Jersey waters. BRECK P. KENT

Before becoming a wildlife management area, much of this site was farmland. Today, approximately 500 acres of the Pequest Wildlife Management Area is leased to local farmers who continue to grow grain. The farmers follow conservation plans to prevent soil erosion and maintain water quality. They also leave a percentage of their crop for wildlife. The remaining acreage is returning naturally to upland forests made up mainly of mixed hardwoods. The combination of upland and streamside forests, brushy old fields, emerging forests, and active cropland supports a great diversity of wildlife.

Hiking trails through fields and upland forests start from the center picnic area. A guide to three marked trails is available in the Natural Resource Education Center. Along the trails, look for white-tailed deer, American goldfinches, wild turkeys, eastern chipmunks, and hawks, depending on the season. Also, look for the bat and bluebird houses near the center, which provide homes for bats, swallows, wrens, and eastern bluebirds.

The area's farmland and forest-edge animals include ring-necked pheasants, raccoons, woodchucks, eastern cottontails, and coyotes; but birds are more visibly active during daylight hours—look for American goldfinches and eastern bluebirds. Bluebirds are insect-eaters and begin their nesting season in March. Goldfinches eat seeds and wait until July to nest, when a favorite plant, thistle, is available to provide nesting material and seeds for food. OPEN FOR HUNTING DURING PRESCRIBED SEASONS.

Directions: *From Route 80, take exit 19 onto County Route 517 south. Drive 5 miles, to Hackettstown. Turn right onto N.J. Route 46 west and travel 8 miles to the hatchery entrance on the left.*

Ownership: NJDEP, Division of Fish, Game, and Wildlife (908) 637-4125

Size: 2,303 acres   **Closest Town:** Oxford, Warren County

Since its reintroduction by New Jersey Division of Fish, Game, and Wildlife in 1977, the state's wild turkey population has grown to over 12,500 birds. RAY DAVIS

6. WORTHINGTON STATE FOREST

Description: Located at the southern end of the Delaware Water Gap National Recreation Area, the state forest lands along the Kittatinny Ridge are mixed deciduous and evergreen.

Viewing Information: Some of the most rugged terrain and splendid views in New Jersey are found in Worthington State Forest. A steep, rocky trail follows Dunnfield Creek from the Delaware River to Mount Tammany and provides a spectacular view of the water gap. Walk the Appalachian Trail to Sunfish Pond for an easy to moderate hike. Birding in the spring and summer and hawk-watching in the fall are excellent. In mixed-oak sections of the woods, look for gray and red squirrels, wild turkeys, and white-tailed deer. OPEN FOR HUNTING DURING PRESCRIBED SEASONS.

Directions: *Traveling west on Interstate 80, take exit 1, the last exit in New Jersey. Turn right on Old Mine Road and travel 3 miles to the state forest entrance on your left. Stop at the office for trail maps and information.*

Ownership: NJDEP, Division of Parks and Forestry (908) 841-9575

Size: 5,878 acres   **Closest Town:** Columbia

7. MERRILL CREEK RESERVOIR

Description: The 650-acre Merrill Creek Reservoir on Scotts Mountain was constructed to store water for release into the Delaware River during periods of low flow. The reservoir is surrounded by more than 2,000 acres of forest and fields. A 290-acre wildlife preserve, with 5 miles of hiking trails, features oak forest, open fields, abandoned orchards, and stands of spruce and pine.

Viewing Information: The 5.5-mile perimeter trail offers excellent views of fall and winter waterfowl. There are two observation blinds, one along the shoreline and the other on the edge of a field. The reservoir is easily accessible by car and is a good spot for hawk-watching during the fall migration or bald eagle-watching during winter months. The Eagle Trail is 0.3-mile long and barrier-free. Ask at the visitor center for a bird checklist.

Directions: *Take NJ 57 west from Washington (Warren County) 7 miles to CR 519 North. Turn right onto CR 519 and proceed approximately 2.5 miles to Fox Farm Road. Turn right on Fox Farm Road and proceed to the stop sign. At the stop sign, turn right onto Richline Road and continue to Merrill Creek Road. Take a right onto Merrill Creek Road and follow the signs to the visitor center.*

Ownership: Merrill Creek Owners Group; Merrill Creek Visitors Center (908) 454-1213

Size: 3,000 acres   **Closest Town:** Washington

HIGHLANDS REGION

This region of rough, mountainous terrain also has areas of rolling hills and farmland, meadows and grassland, and prime beaver habitat. It contains the highest concentration of glacial lakes in the state, or the entire Eastern Seaboard, for that matter. There are also numerous reservoirs, lakes, and ponds that were created when many of the region's rivers and streams were dammed.

An array of habitats occur on the ridges and valleys that dominate the landscape here. These include pitch pine–scrub oak forests; hemlock ravines; northern mixed–hardwood forests of oak, maple, birch, ash, hickory, hemlock, and white pine; and old farm fields and woodlots in various stages of succession. The large contiguous forest of the Highlands supports the highest concentration of birds of prey in the state—Cooper's hawks, goshawks, barred owls, and red-shouldered hawks nest throughout the forests of this region, along with many songbirds that rely on deep forest for successful reproduction. Large flocks of wild turkeys and herds of white-tailed deer roam the forests and fields, as do coyotes, bears, and bobcats. Black bears and bobcats are denizens of the many rhododendron and mountain laurel swamps that dot the higher elevation's landscape.

The Highlands also contain thousands of acres of glacial, floodplain, and spring-fed wetlands, which feed its numerous streams. Beavers, otters, great blue herons, and endangered and threatened species, including bog turtles and

wood turtles, depend on the extensive network of wetlands, lakes, and streams. This region also supports large populations of small mammals, reptiles, amphibians, butterflies, moths, and dragonflies.

The Highlands Region's huge areas of public land are an anomaly in New Jersey—the Great Swamp National Wildlife Refuge, Waywayanda, Ringwood, Longpond Ironworks state parks, the Pyramid Mountain Natural Historical Area, the 35,000-acre Pequannock Watershed (owned by the city of Newark but open by permit to the public), the Black River and Wildcat Ridge wildlife management areas, and many other state, county, and municipal tracts provide large expanses of contiguous natural lands. This preservation of entire ecosystems benefits wildlife and allows for extended hikes and pleasing vistas from many vantage points.

Visitors to this region will also delight in the many historical and cultural features that the Highlands have to offer. Rich deposits of iron led to the development of ironworks and "plantations" as early as the 1760s. Ringwood, Longpond, Andover, Oxford, and numerous other locations were the sites of furnaces, forges, and bloomeries. Many of the furnaces and buildings are still standing. There are also many historical sites associated with the American Revolution, including those in and around Morristown, such as Jockey Hollow and the Ford Mansion. The Morris Canal, in operation for 100 years, beginning in 1823, traversed the region, leaving behind its inclined planes and locks in Waterloo Village and the portless towns of Port Murray and Port Colden.

Above: *River otters hunt for fish in the many glacial lakes and wetlands of the Highlands. Although they usually remain in or close to streams and wetlands, they will travel overland to reach other habitat.* LEONARD LEE RUE III

Preceding page: *New Jersey's Highlands region is home to the largest unfragmented northern hardwood forests remaining in the state. These forests provide critical habitat for black bear, red-shouldered hawks, timber rattlesnakes, and migratory songbirds.* DWIGHT HISCANO

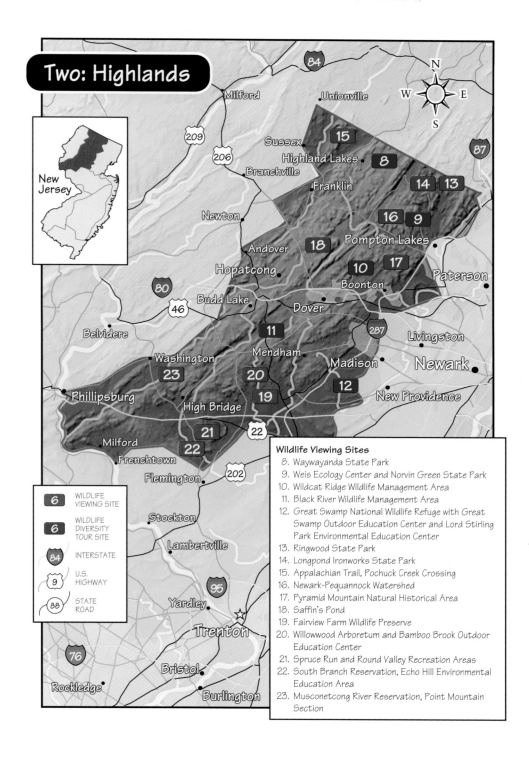

Two: Highlands

New Jersey

Wildlife Viewing Sites

8. Waywayanda State Park
9. Weis Ecology Center and Norvin Green State Park
10. Wildcat Ridge Wildlife Management Area
11. Black River Wildlife Management Area
12. Great Swamp National Wildlife Refuge with Great Swamp Outdoor Education Center and Lord Stirling Park Environmental Education Center
13. Ringwood State Park
14. Longpond Ironworks State Park
15. Appalachian Trail, Pochuck Creek Crossing
16. Newark-Pequannock Watershed
17. Pyramid Mountain Natural Historical Area
18. Saffin's Pond
19. Fairview Farm Wildlife Preserve
20. Willowwood Arboretum and Bamboo Brook Outdoor Education Center
21. Spruce Run and Round Valley Recreation Areas
22. South Branch Reservation, Echo Hill Environmental Education Area
23. Musconetcong River Reservation, Point Mountain Section

WILDLIFE VIEWING SITE

WILDLIFE DIVERSITY TOUR SITE

INTERSTATE

U.S. HIGHWAY

STATE ROAD

GREEN-BACKED HERON

WOODCOCK

GREAT SWAMP

WOOD DUCK

BARRED OWL

LOON

EASTERN KINGBIRD

PILEATED WOODPECKER

RATTLESNAKE

MONARCH BUTTERFLY

The Highlands Region's glacial lakes and kettle hole ponds are hotbeds of animal activity. Migratory waterfowl use them for resting and refueling, feeding on seeds and roots. At night, the lakes provide protection for waterfowl that raft-up far from shore to stay safe from predators. In warmer months, birds can be seen swooping above the water surface, catching emerging insects. Herons hunt the shallows for fish and frogs while river otters fish the depths. Many species of wild-

BEAVER

RIVER OTTER

RED-SHOULDERED HAWK

BEAVERLODGE

CANADA GOOSE

COYOTE

PORCUPINE

WHITE-TAILED DEER

SPOTTED TURTLE

life, including coyotes and white-tailed deer, come to the lake to drink. Barred owls and red-shouldered hawks nest deep within the large, swampy forests.

As lakes mature, they gradually fill in, growing smaller and shallower as the collar of vegetation around them tightens. Eventually, the lake will become a bog, then a meadow, then a forest.

8. WAYWAYANDA STATE PARK

Description: Enjoy the captivating scenery of the northern highlands while hiking miles of marked trails. Located along the New York state border, atop the Waywayanda Plateau, nearly a third of this park is preserved in three natural areas—Bearfort Mountain, Waywayanda Swamp, and Waywayanda Hemlock Ravine. The remains of buildings from a once-thriving iron-making village surround a furnace that was last used in 1843. A 19.6-mile section of the Appalachian Trail travels through the varied terrain of the park.

Diversity Tour Information: Waywayanda's northern hardwood forests and large patches of contiguous, forested cover are very important habitat for many species of wildlife, including several of New Jersey's threatened and endangered raptors, including barred owls, Cooper's hawks, and red-shouldered hawks. Much of the raptors' habitat in the northern part of the state has been impacted by development in recent years, making the long-term stewardship of the park's northern hardwood forest ecosystem all the more critical. Public lands like this one are key to the long-term survival of viable populations of species that need mature, unfragmented forest.

The park is critical habitat for black bears, bobcats, porcupines, coyotes, and foxes, as well as wild turkeys, ruffed grouse, and pileated woodpeckers. The elusive bobcat roams the rocky ridges and hunts the forests and swamps year-round. The Division of Fish, Game, and Wildlife caught and released bobcats from New England on Bearfort Mountain, in the early 1980s, in an effort

The secretive bobcat is a true symbol of New Jersey's remaining wilderness. Biologists are actively monitoring the state's population, which has been growing steadily since 22 cats were introduced in the early 1980s. JEFF LEPORE

to restore New Jersey's dwindling population. Although listed as an endangered species, the bobcat population in New Jersey appears to be growing.

New Jersey's population of black bears is estimated at 550 animals, and of these, probably 25–30 reside in, or pass through, Waywayanda State Park each year. You may have to look no further than the visitor center to see black bears. Bears are seen in the park from late March through December. During the winter months, they hibernate in dens that they make in hollow logs or caves, under windfalls or brush piles, or in nests they create in rhododendron thickets. Waywayanda's northern hardwood forest, with its varied terrain, meets all of a bear's needs for food and cover .

In addition to being important habitat for bobcats and black bears, the wetlands in the park are home to many less-reclusive species, including beavers, otters, and great blue herons. The park has a heron rookery, where the great blue herons nest high in the trees, in large stick nests. The nesting herons and their offspring are often seen feeding in the wetlands and various bodies of water throughout the park. Herons employ a "wade and wait" method of fishing, letting the fish come to them. When the fish realize that the heron's shadow is alive, they veer away instinctively, but it is too late! The heron uncoils its great neck, driving its daggerlike bill down to snap shut on its prey. The park's large population of fish-eating herons is a good indication that it is a healthy aquatic ecosystem.

Beavers also thrive in Waywayanda's wetlands. To see their handiwork, you need look no further than the downed trees by the side of the road in the Waywayanda Swamp Natural Area, or the beaver sign visible from the bridge on the Double Pond Trail.

The Waywayanda Hemlock Ravine Natural Area is a steep, shaded hemlock forest surrounded by mixed-oak and hardwood forests. Look here to see red-eyed vireo, blackburnian warblers, scarlet tanagers, black-capped chickadees, and tufted titmice feeding in the forest canopy.

The great blue heron is listed as a threatened species in New Jersey. The breeding population is in danger due to loss and fragmentation of its forest habitat. CHARLES H. WILLEY

Eastern hemlock needles are quite acidic, accumulating in a cushiony mat on the forest floor instead of breaking down to become part of the soil. The only plants that can break through this thick, acidic layer are members of the heath family, like the blueberries and rhododendrons that you see here.

Hemlocks provide feeding and nesting sites for many species of wildlife, as well as shelter from the wind. Their cones are a source of food and the insects attracted to the trees' boughs are a feast for many birds. The hemlock forest floor remains moist year-round, thanks to the shade of the larger trees. This moist realm is home to lungless salamanders, which need moist skin to breathe. The hemlock forests also have a surprising number of shrews and moles that feed on the abundance of amphibians and insects that like the cool, damp environment.

Several of New Jersey's threatened birds, including red-shouldered hawks and barred owls, as well as endangered reptiles, including timber rattlesnakes and wood turtles, are found in the Bearfort Mountain Natural Area. Take the Terrace Pond trails from Clinton Road to see this area's mixed-oak hardwood forest, swamp, scrub oak forest, and rocky terrain.

OPEN FOR HUNTING IN DESIGNATED AREAS DURING PRESCRIBED SEASONS.

Directions: *From County Route 513 (Union Valley Road) in West Milford, go north to White Road. Turn left and proceed on White Road 0.2 mile to Warwick Turnpike. Turn left (north) on Warwick Turnpike and travel 6 miles to the park entrance (on the left).*

Wildlife Diversity Tour Directions:

FROM WAYWAYANDA STATE PARK (SITE 8) TO WEIS ECOLOGY CENTER (SITE 9)

From the Waywayanda State Park office, take Warwick Turnpike south until it joins County Route 511. Continue on CR 511 south for several miles to West Brook Road. Turn right on West Brook Road and proceed for 2 miles to Snake Den Road. Turn left (south) and go 0.7 mile, staying left at the fork, to the entrance of Weis Ecology Center.

Ownership: NJDEP Division of Parks and Forestry (973) 853-4462

Size: 13,000 acres   **Closest Town:** West Milford

The *"who cooks for you"* call of the barred owl resounds at night through the forests of places like Waywayanda. This large owl requires mature forests that provide suitable nesting trees and an open understory for hunting.

SIMON B. LEVENTHAL

9. WEIS ECOLOGY CENTER AND NORVIN GREEN STATE PARK

Description: Explore New Jersey's spectacular Highlands region as you hike through mixed-hardwood forests, along rocky ridges, beside cascading waterfalls and past cultural features. The Roomy Mine, in Norvin Green State Forest, is an old, abandoned iron mine that is open to the public for exploration. A 360-degree vantage point at Wyanokie High Point presents a sweeping panorama of the nearby Wanaque Reservoir. Chikahoki Falls and the mixed oak-hemlock ravine are equally beautiful. The Weis Ecology Center, run by the New Jersey Audubon Society and open to the public, has programs, workshops, and other events on weekends and evenings.

Diversity Tour Information: This is a Diversity Tour site where you could spend a full day or even an entire weekend. The park abounds with wildlife viewing opportunities and interesting countryside. Start with bald eagle and osprey viewing over Wanaque Reservoir. The creation of a long-term, secure water supply for New Jersey's cities, at Wanaque and other nearby reservoirs, has led to the protection of important habitats for osprey and eagles. Development of the reservoir system has resulted in not only a tremendous increase in watershed protection and water quality improvements, but also in the creation of nesting and feeding habitat for these large birds of prey and many other species of wildlife. Just over the state line in New York, but still part of the Wanaque watershed, the Sterling Forest also provides important water quality protection.

As a result of reintroduction efforts by the NJDEP and DFGW on northern New Jersey lakes, ospreys are believed to nest in this area. To restore ospreys to the inland waters where they had nested in the past, biologists conducted a hacking project from 1985–1989, releasing 36 young ospreys on the Wanaque Reservoir and other lakes in the area. Bald eagles have nested near Wanaque Reservoir since the early 1990s, although the exact location of their nest is not known. An adult pair has been sighted at the Reservoir during breeding season

A forest dweller, the ovenbird gets its name from the oven-shaped nest it builds on the forest floor. Listen for its loud, rising "teacher, teacher, teacher, TEACHER" call. TOM VEZO

HIGHLANDS

every year since 1990. Ospreys and eagles are proven indicators of environmental quality. Feeding largely on fish, their health reflects the quality of a food source shared by humans.

The 2700-plus-acre Norvin Green State Forest offers splendid hiking on 23 miles of trails and wildlife viewing opportunities in the characteristically rugged terrain and mixed-oak forests of the New Jersey Highlands region. These forested ecosystems provide an excellent opportunity to see white-tailed deer, black bears, bobcats, red and gray foxes, striped skunks, Virginia opossums, and many songbirds and raptors. In particular, look for the many kinds of warblers that breed and nest in the deep woods.

The Weis Ecology Center, situated on 160 acres, was created to offer the public a unique opportunity to learn about the Highlands region. The center is open Wednesday through Sunday. Be sure to pick up a checklist of Highlands birds and a trail map. For camping adventures, there are wooded campsites and rustic cabins available for rental, by reservation only. Visitors are invited to use the center's picnic tables, nestled near a Norway spruce grove adjacent to the parking area.

The center's well-marked trails lead to diverse locations around the center and throughout Norvin Green State Forest. Take the Blue Trail to enjoy a scenic view of the Wanaque Reservoir from Wyanokie High Point. The High Point is a 900-foot cliff rising dramatically from the valley below. This semi-challenging climb is well worth the effort—visitors are rewarded with a truly breathtaking view in all directions. Usually, there are red-tailed hawks or turkey vultures soaring above this point. Occasionally, you may also spot a bald eagle or an osprey.

The White Trail is a big loop trail that leads through the southern quarter of the state park, through mixed-oak hardwood forests, to the most spectacu-

Though white-tailed deer were nearly eliminated from New Jersey during the 1800s, the state now boasts a herd of around 150,000. LEN RUE, JR.

lar portion of the Chikahoki Falls. Look and listen for Louisiana and northern water thrushes, blackburnian warblers, and red-eyed vireos, along the trail.

The Yellow or Red trails will take you to the Roomy Mine, which, since being abandoned, has become a year-round home for bats. Several species of bat, including little brown, big brown, and red, as well as eastern pipistrels, are known to hibernate in the mine from mid-November through mid-February. Visitors are asked not to enter the mine during this period, to avoid disturbing the bats. During the rest of the year, the best bat-viewing time at the mine is during midday or at dusk when the bats leave to feed on insects in the nearby forest.

OPEN FOR HUNTING DURING PRESCRIBED SEASONS.

Directions: *From Interstate 287, Exit 55 in Wanaque, take County Route 511 north for 3.8 miles to West Brook Road. The road is not marked from the south. Turn left (west) and travel for 2 miles on West Brook Road to Snake Den Road. Turn left (south) on Snake Den Road and go 0.7 mile, staying left at the fork, to the Weis Ecology Center entrance.*

Wildlife Diversity Tour Directions:
FROM WEIS ECOLOGY CENTER (SITE 9)
TO WILDCAT RIDGE WILDLIFE MANAGEMENT AREA (SITE 10)

From Weis Ecology Center, take Snake Den Road 0.7 mile to West Brook Road. Turn right on West Brook Road and travel 2 miles to County Route 511. Take CR 511 south to Interstate 287. Proceed south on I-287 to Interstate 80 west. Stay on I-80 west to exit 37. Travel north on County Route 513 toward Hibernia for 2.8 miles. Turn right on Sunnyside Road. Parking area for Wildcat Ridge WMA trail is immediately on the left.

Ownership: Weis Ecology Center: New Jersey Audubon Society (973) 835-2160. Norvin Green State Forest: NJDEP Division of Parks and Forestry (973) 962-7031

Size: Weis Ecology Center 160 acres, Norvin Green State Forest 2,789 acres

Closest Town: Ringwood

The yellow warbler's bright yellow color and rust-streaked breast make it easy to identify.
SIMON B. LEVENTHAL

10. WILDCAT RIDGE WILDLIFE MANAGEMENT AREA

Description: Thousands of bats hibernate through winter in a former iron mine at the foot of the ridge. Hiking trails and overlooks on the upper section of the ridge provide unparalleled views of the forested ridges and lush valleys of the Highlands.

Diversity Tour Information: The Hibernia Mine, in the Wildcat Ridge Wildlife Management Area, is the state's largest known bat hibernaculum. In July of 1994, New Jersey Division of Fish, Game, and Wildlife biologists, in cooperation with the U.S. Fish and Wildlife Service and Bat Conservation International, erected a gate to protect the more than 26,000 bats that hibernate annually in the abandoned Hibernia Mine.

Park at the lower lot off Sunnyside Road for an easy five-minute walk to the gated entrance of the former mine. You will feel the cool air coming from the mine before you see the entrance. The mine is inhabited year-round by male bats and nonbreeding females. The hibernating species are primarily little brown bats, with a small number of big brown bats, eastern pipistrels, and state and federally endangered Indiana bats. Indiana bats (*Myotis sodalis*) resemble the common little brown bat, but are more uniformly pinkish brown with pinkish lips and nose. In the summer, Indiana bats forage in wooded or semiwooded areas along streams and often roost in the space beneath loose bark on hickory or maple trees.

During the fall, thousands of mating bats swarm about the mine entrance in the evenings, the prelude to winter hibernation. Bats are active again at the mine entrance on spring evenings after emerging from hibernation. For the protection of the bats and because of wildlife management area regulations, the area is closed from dusk until dawn. An observation platform with interpretive signs is planned for construction near the mine entrance. Call (908) 735-8975 for information on guided evening observation programs.

There are several trails beginning near the mine parking area that lead to the ridge and the upper portion of the property. An alternative to hiking to the top is driving to the trailhead for Beaver Pond Trail or the Overlook Trail (see directions below).

Beaver-created wetlands are focal points for many other wildlife species, including muskrats, otters, and raccoons. The importance of beaver ponds to waterfowl can not be overstated. Mallards, wood ducks, and black ducks thrive in these small woodland wetlands, as do many reptiles and amphibians. In addition to their value to waterfowl, beaver ponds provide critical habitat for bluebirds and tree swallows, which nest in the cavities of dead and dying trees. Also, beaver ponds provide feeding grounds for herons and kingfishers.

Continue past the Beaver Pond Trail parking area to the Overlook Trail for a spectacular vista of the forests and valleys of the Highlands. On a clear day, the New York City skyline is visible from this overlook high on the edge of the ridge. This is also a great place to see migrating hawks, in the spring and fall, as they ride the thermals along the ridgetop. In fact, this is one of the Hawk Migration Association of North America's official hawk counting stations, manned by an association volunteer nearly every day during spring and fall.

The breathtaking view of the Highlands is well worth the walk to the lookout, with or without the hawks. The view provides an otherwise hard-to-obtain understanding of the vastness of the Highlands. No other area in north Jersey has the contiguous tracts of forest necessary to preserve healthy populations of endangered hawks, owls, and increasingly rare songbirds.

Wildcat Ridge Wildlife Management Area is a natural area with no facilities. ENTERING THE HIBERNIA MINE IS PROHIBITED. AREA OPEN FOR HUNTING DURING PRESCRIBED SEASONS.

Directions: *From Interstate 80, take Exit 37. Travel north on County Route 513 toward Hibernia for 2.8 miles. Turn right on Sunnyside Road. The parking area is on the left. For the Beaver Pond Trailhead: Continue north on CR 513 for another 3.7 miles. Turn right on Upper Hibernia Road and proceed 2.6 miles to the parking area on the left. For the Overlook Trailhead: Stay on Upper Hibernia Road for 0.2 mile beyond the Beaver Pond Trail parking area; parking for the Overlook Trail is on the right side of the road.*

Wildlife Diversity Tour Directions:
FROM WILDCAT RIDGE WILDLIFE MANAGEMENT AREA (SITE 10)
TO BLACK RIVER WILDLIFE MANAGEMENT AREA (SITE 11)

From Wildcat Ridge WMA, return to County Route 513 south and proceed for approximately 15 miles to the entrance to Black River WMA on the right.

Ownership: NJDEP, Division of Fish, Game, and Wildlife (908) 637-4125

Size: 2,653 acres   **Closest Town:** Hibernia

The former Hibernia mine at Wildcat Ridge is the winter home of 25,000 little brown bats. The bats need the constant temperature found in underground caves to slow down their metabolism to the point where they can survive the entire winter on stored body fat. DR. PETER J. LEKOS

11. BLACK RIVER WILDLIFE MANAGEMENT AREA

Description: The Black River is nestled in a valley of small farms and large suburban lots. The contiguous, wild vegetation of the Black River WMA is riparian habitat—a linear greenway for wildlife. The meandering river and its extensive freshwater marsh, next to upland forests and fields, contain a wide assortment of wildlife.

Diversity Tour Information: An abundance of breeding and feeding species awaits the visitor to both of the area's viewing sites.

The long "edge habitat," the interface between land and water, of the Black River provides the largest contiguous parcel of habitat remaining in this part of the region and is an important corridor for wildlife travel. In addition to cover, this corridor provides easy access to drinking water, protected sites for dens and nests, and sunny spots for berries and other fruit-producing shrubs to grow. The muddy wetland edges are great places to look for the tracks of upland mammals and birds that visit the river. Deer come to drink and, at night, mink and raccoons come down to hunt for crayfish and turtle eggs. Belted kingfishers dive from perches at the water's edge to catch fish, and river otters slide down the banks and dive for fish in the moving water.

River otters are active year-round, especially from dawn to midmorning and again in the evening. They swim with the top of their head and eyes out of the water, trailing a V-shaped wake behind them. Otters have a fast metabolism that burns food quickly, so they must eat up to four times a day.

The Black River Valley forms a natural travelway for people as well as wildlife. The first settlers to northern New Jersey, and Revolutionary War troops, walked these pathways more than 200 years ago. Later, people and goods moved through this valley on horseback and by railroad. The old railroad bed has been converted to a foot trail. Hike the 3-plus-mile section that parallels

Mink prefer edge habitat along streams and rivers, where they can find ample food and shelter. They make their dens near the water, under tree roots, bank undercuts, or in old beaver bank dens. JEFF LEPORE

the Black River. This trail provides some of the best opportunities to view freshwater wetland, forested ecosystem wildlife, and riparian habitat. Parking for the rail trail is at the Pleasant Hill Road parking area (see directions).

Another good way to view wildlife in the Black River Valley is from the river itself. Launch a canoe upstream on Pleasant Hill Road and take a leisurely 3-mile paddle to the take-out point in the wildlife management area parking lot (see directions). All of Black River is popular with canoeists, who also refer to the river as the Lamington River. Just downstream from the wildlife management area, the Black River flows through Hacklebarney State Park. The shallow, slow-moving stream is perfect for a lazy summer afternoon outing.

In the fields-and-forests portion of the wildlife management area, look for blue-winged and chestnut-sided warblers. Spring migration is a particularly good time to see warblers. Park in the parking area for the wildlife management area off of County Route 513. Look for white-tailed deer feeding in shrubby areas at dawn and dusk.

The NJDEP/DFGW is not managing this area to provide habitat solely for warblers, but also for other songbirds and a variety of other species—white-tailed deer, wild turkeys, and red-tailed hawks. Some of the habitat management involves the provision or enhancement of low-growing food supplies, escape cover, and winter shelter. Fields are used by deer and many other species, so managers maintain the open space by mowing or brush-hogging. Agricultural crops such as alfalfa, hay, and corn are also planted by area farmers who lease the land and are required to leave a portion of their crops for wildlife.

The Black River WMA is a natural area with no facilities. OPEN FOR HUNTING DURING PRESCRIBED SEASONS.

Directions: *From US Highway 206 in Chester, take County Route 513 north, proceeding 1 mile to traffic light. Follow CR 513 straight for 1.8 miles to the WMA entrance on the left. The entrance is at the southern edge of a large parking area. For access to the Black River, proceed as above and at traffic light, turn left onto Oakdale Road. At the stop sign, turn right onto Pleasant Hill Road. Travel 0.2 mile to the parking area on the right before the river. The parking area is the trailhead for the old railroad trail. The canoe takeout parking area is 0.2 mile past the railroad trail parking area, on the left after you cross the river. To launch a canoe, travel 4.1 miles further on Pleasant Hill Road. Parking lot and river access are on the right. ROADSIDE PARKING IS PROHIBITED IN CHESTER TOWNSHIP.*

Wildlife Diversity Tour Directions:

FROM BLACK RIVER WILDLIFE MANAGEMENT AREA (SITE 11) TO SOMERSET COUNTY PARK COMMISSION ENVIRONMENTAL EDUCATION CENTER (SITE 12)

From Black River WMA, take County Route 513 south to U.S. Highway 206 south. Proceed to U.S. Highway 202 east. Follow US 202 east through Far Hills and Bernardsville to North Maple Avenue. Turn left on North Maple Avenue and proceed for 3.5 miles to Lord Stirling Road. Turn left and travel 1 mile to Somerset County Park Commission Environmental Education Center on the left.

Ownership: NJDEP, Division of Fish, Game, and Wildlife (908) 637-4125

Size: 3,071 acres   **Closest Towns:** Chester, Chester Township

Description: The Great Swamp Area encompasses the Great Swamp National Wildlife Refuge, the Great Swamp Outdoor Education Center of Morris County Park Commission, and the Somerset County Park Commission Environmental Education Center at Lord Stirling Park. The swamp is a remnant of the ancient glacial Lake Passaic, which once occupied much of the current day Passaic River floodplain. Today, its marshes, ponds, hardwood swamps, and upland forests host a variety of wildlife. All three sites offer special events and exhibits interpreting the wildlife and habitats of the area—call for specific program information. The National Wildlife Refuge features a wildlife tour route for automobiles, 0.5 mile of boardwalk trails, and two observation blinds. Educational programs offered at the Lord Stirling Park Center and the Great Swamp Outdoor Education Center enrich visitors' understanding of the swamp ecosystem.

Diversity Tour Information: The best season to see marsh and water birds in the Great Swamp is during early spring migration, before vegetation emerges to hide them. The refuge has great populations of nesting wood ducks and bluebirds, thanks to the hundreds of nest boxes maintained for both species. Other noteworthy residents are red-shouldered hawks, red-tailed hawks, barred owls, and great blue herons. Summer also offers good wildlife viewing opportunities, but beware of the biting insects.

The Great Swamp National Wildlife Refuge was established to provide migration, nesting, and feeding habitat for migratory birds in an area where

habitats for many species are highly fragmented due to development. Great Swamp contains more than 7,400 acres of hardwood swamp, upland timber, marsh, brush, pasture, and cropland. This diverse habitat attracts a wide variety of migratory and resident birds. With the continued protection of its wilderness, the National Wildlife Refuge will become increasingly important as a haven for wildlife amidst the surrounding urban areas.

The swamp contains many old oak and beech trees, red maple, stands of mountain laurel, and species of other plants from both the northern and southern botanical zones. The National Wildlife Refuge hosts more than 220 species of birds in various seasons. Its mammals include white-tailed deer, river otters, muskrats, raccoons, skunks, red foxes, woodchucks, gray squirrels, opossums, and eastern cottontails; and there are an interesting variety of fish, reptiles, and amphibians, including wood turtles, eastern and midland painted turtles, and endangered bog turtles. The endangered blue-spotted salamander is also found on the National Wildlife Refuge. This is one of the few places in New Jersey where the blue-spotted salamander still exists.

The western half of the National Wildlife Refuge is intensively managed to maintain optimum habitat for a wide variety of wildlife. Water levels are regulated, grasslands and brush are mowed periodically to maintain habitat and species diversity, shrubs are planted, nesting structures are provided, and other habitat management practices are employed. Public access in this area is limited to the Wildlife Observation Center and Pleasant Plains Road to minimize disturbance to wildlife.

Numerous wetland raptors inhabit the Swamp. Look closely to catch a glimpse of the courtship rituals of barred owls or red-shouldered hawks. One good place to start is the 897-acre Lord Stirling Park, which occupies the western portion of the Great Swamp Basin. Lord Stirling Park's Environmental Education Center offers an 8.5-mile trail system, including 2.5 miles of boardwalk, allowing easy access to wetter portions of the park. Naturalists are available to answer questions and provide information, and an extensive range of programs is offered.

Explore the 40-acre Great Swamp Outdoor

The wood duck nests in tree cavities, unlike the many species of duck that nest on the ground. Hundreds of nest boxes have been erected throughout the Great Swamp Wetlands to simulate tree cavities, which wood ducks need to nest. CLAY MYERS

Preceding page: *The thousands of acres of wetland in the Great Swamp National Wildlife Refuge are the remnants of Great Glacial Lake Passaic, which covered vast portions of four New Jersey counties in prehistoric times.*
JOHN AND KAREN HOLLINGSWORTH

Education Center located in the eastern portion of the Great Swamp. The center adjoins the National Wildlife Refuge. There are guided nature walks on the grounds of the center and in the refuge. Inside the center, visitors will find informative exhibits, plus many interactive games for kids, trail guides, and listings of programs. GREAT SWAMP NATIONAL WILDLIFE REFUGE IS OPEN FOR LIMITED HUNTING.

Directions: *From Interstate 287 Exit 30A (Maple Avenue), travel 3 miles to Lord Stirling Road. Turn left. Somerset County Park Commission Environmental Education Center is 1 mile farther on the left. For Great Swamp National Wildlife Refuge, continue on Lord Stirling Road (which becomes White Bridge Road). Turn left on Pleasant Plains Road and proceed through the gate to refuge headquarters on the right. For the Great Swamp Outdoor Education Center of the Morris County Park Commission, continue on Pleasant Plains Road to White Bridge Road. Turn left and proceed to New Vernon Road. Turn right and travel to Meyersville Road. Turn left and proceed 2.4 miles on Meyersville Road to Fairmount Road. Turn left on Fairmount and proceed 1.8 miles to Southern Boulevard. Turn left and go 1 mile to entrance on the left.*

Ownership: National Wildlife Refuge: U.S. Fish and Wildlife Service (973) 425-1222; Great Swamp Outdoor Education Center: Morris County Park Commission (973) 635-6629; Somerset County Park Commission Environmental Education Center at Lord Stirling Park (908) 766-2489

Size: National Wildlife Refuge 7,400 acres, Morris County Center 40 acres, Somerset County Center 430 acres

Closest Towns: Stirling, Chatham, and Basking Ridge

The Virginia oppossum is North America's most primitive, yet common, mammal. A marsupial, it carries its young in its pouch for the first three months. After that, they ride on their mother's back until old enough to keep up with her. LEN RUE, JR.

13. RINGWOOD STATE PARK

Description: Development of Ringwood's iron industry began in 1740. America's foremost ironmaster, Abram S. Hewitt, built Ringwood Manor, a National Historical Landmark. The gardens surrounding Skylands Manor House are the only botanical gardens in the state park system. Notable natural habitats include a northern New Jersey shrub swamp, hardwood-conifer swamp, and ridgetop communities of plants specifically adapted to the extremely dry, harsh conditions existing on rocky outcrops and cliffs.

Viewing Informwation: These vast, contiguous forests, connecting other state parks and forests to Ringwood, are good habitat for black bears, wild turkeys, and endangered bobcats. Bobcats are wary of humans and are more often heard than seen. Bald eagles frequent the region, which is noted for its many lakes. Canada geese are plentiful around Sally's Pond, near the park office. Park at Skylands Manor for trails. A trail map is available at the office or toll booth. OPEN FOR HUNTING IN DESIGNATED AREAS DURING PRESCRIBED SEASONS.

Directions: *From County Route 511 in Bloomingdale, travel north on CR 511 for 8.5 miles to Sloatsburg Road. Turn right and travel 1.5 miles to the park entrance sign. Continue for 1.1 miles to the office at Ringwood Manor.*

Ownership: NJDEP Division of Parks and Forestry (973) 962-7031

Size: 4,291 acres   **Closest Town:** Ringwood

14. LONGPOND IRONWORKS STATE PARK

Description: A reservoir, trout stream, and hemlock forest make this historical area a great wildlife viewing site.

Viewing Information: A panoply of bird life frequents the state park year-round. Take the trails from the parking lot by Monksville Reservoir up into the forest. Watch for porcupines, coyotes, white-tailed deer, and black bears from March to December. Pileated woodpeckers, wild turkeys, red-shouldered hawks, Cooper's hawks, and spring and summer warblers are just a few of the birds to be seen. In fall and winter, check the reservoir for waterfowl.
OPEN FOR HUNTING DURING PRESCRIBED SEASONS.

Directions: *From the junction of county routes 513 and 511, just north of West Milford, take CR 511 (Greenwood Lake Turnpike) east for 4.3 miles to the park entrance on the right.*

Ownership: NJDEP Division of Parks and Forestry (973) 962-7031

Size: 1,729 acres   **Closest Town:** West Milford

15. APPALACHIAN TRAIL–POCHUK CREEK CROSSING

Description: New Jersey was the first state to acquire a continuous protected Appalachian Trail corridor. By 1998, a new trail connecting the Pochuk Creek bridge with County Route 517 and Canal Road will cross open, low-lying wetlands and mixed-oak woodlands. It will also allow those who cannot complete the entire 2,000 miles of the Appalachian Trail to enjoy a part of it.

Viewing Information: The elevated suspension bridge across the Pochuk Creek's quagmire is a perfect viewing platform. Northern harriers soar overhead, or even at eye-level, looking for small rodents, like voles, for prey. A barred owl might hunt the same meadowlike area at dusk and during the night. Eastern phoebes swoop over the wetland in search of insects. Tracks of raccoons, white-tailed deer, and great blue herons are seen in the mud. Pochuk Creek crossing is a natural area with no facilities.

Directions: *From the junction of County Route 517 and Maple Grange Road, take CR 517 north for approximately 1 mile to the Appalachian Trail Crossing.*

Ownership: NJDEP Division of Parks and Forestry and National Park Service; contact management partner, the New York–New Jersey Trail Conference (212) 685-9699

Size: N/A   **Closest Town:** Vernon

16. NEWARK–PEQUANNOCK WATERSHED

Description: Located within 35 miles of the New Jersey–New York metropolitan area, the watershed encompasses nearly 35,000 acres of open space. Its five reservoirs provide water for the city of Newark and many recreational opportunities. Several miles of trails wind through the varied, often rocky, terrain.

Viewing Information: The watershed provides niches for numerous forest-dwelling birds and mammals. Scan the tree-tops for dozing porcupines. Wild turkeys, ruffed grouse, white-tailed deer, and gray squirrels feed on the area's abundant acorns. Black bears love blueberries, as do raccoons, red foxes, and numerous species of birds. Call or visit the Echo Lake office for information and to purchase an access permit before visiting the site. ACCESS PERMITS ARE REQUIRED. OPEN FOR HUNTING DURING PRESCRIBED SEASONS.

Directions: *From the junction of Interstate 287 and New Jersey 23, take NJ 23 north for almost 8 miles to Echo Lake Road. Turn right and travel 1 mile to the Echo Lake Office on the left.*

Ownership: City of Newark, managed by the Newark Watershed Conservation and Development Corporation, P.O. Box 319, Newfoundland, NJ 07435 (973) 697-2850

Size: 35,000 acres   **Closest Town:** Newfoundland

Description: The mountain provides diverse habitat for 400 species of native plants, more than 100 kinds of birds, and 30 species of mammals. All this is encircled by major highways and within sight of New York City's skyline.

Viewing Information: Five marked trails meander through and around fields, forests, rock outcroppings, streams, and wetlands. The Blue Trail has an over-look with a view of New York City. Look for a famous glacial erratic named Tripod Rock. This huge rock has been balanced on three small boulders for the last 15,000 years. Chestnut oaks, numerous on high ridges, and stands of beech trees, help provide forest cover for year-round residents like pileated woodpeckers, red-bellied woodpeckers, wild turkeys, and black-capped chickadees. Summer neotropical visitors include scarlet tanagers, yellow war-blers, and indigo buntings. As you hike along the trails, you may spot black bears, beavers, white-tailed deer, or coyotes. Bobcats still inhabit the region, too. Cat Swamps and Cat Rocks were named for this shy forest inhabitant.

Directions: *Take County Route 511 north from Main Street in Boonton. Proceed on CR 511 (Boonton Avenue) for 3.3 miles. The visitor center is on the left.*

Ownership: Morris County Park Commission (973) 334-3130

Size: More than 1,000 acres   **Closest Town:** Boonton

HIGHLANDS

Pileated woodpeckers excavate large holes from dead trees for their nests. Both male and female work to hammer out the hole, which may take 30 days to complete. CHARLES H. WILLEY

55

18. SAFFIN'S POND

Description: Saffin's Pond provides access to the large Mahlon Dickerson Reservation, managed by the Morris County Park Commission. Beechwoods, wetlands, and grasslands surround the pond, one of many glacial lakes in the Berkshire Valley area.

Viewing Information: Loop trails begin at the large parking lot. Walk around the pond, no more than a mile, through woods of tulip poplars, sassafras, and rhododendrons. Glacial rocks and boulders, deposited here more than 10,000 years ago, are good perching places for listening to bull frogs and songbirds in the spring. Breeding birds and beavers enliven walking trails in the summer. This is a great place to practice identifying ferns and violets.

Directions: *From Interstate 80, take exit 34B onto New Jersey 15 north. In Hurdtown, just over 4 miles away on NJ 15, take the Weldon Road exit to the east. Continue on Weldon Road for 3.1 miles to the entrance on the right.*

Ownership: Morris County Park Commission (973) 326-7600

Size: Saffin's Pond 1,000 acres, Mahlon Dickerson Reservation 2,689 acres

Closest Town: Oak Ridge

19. FAIRVIEW FARM WILDLIFE PRESERVE

Description: Fairview Farm is an Upper Raritan Watershed Association wildlife preserve. The watershed of the North Branch of the Raritan River and its tributaries comprises 194 square miles in Somerset, Hunterdon, and Morris counties. The 150-acre preserve has an extensive trail system through old farm fields, mowed pastures and lawns, upland conifers and hardwoods, evergreen plantations, and gardens. The office, with restrooms and information, is open only on weekdays.

Viewing Information: June is the nicest season here. It is cool, spring plants are blooming, and there are 75 species of nesting birds to see. Watch for nesting grasshopper sparrows and bobolinks. Near the parking area, the bird-and-butterfly-attracting garden is your first viewing stop. More than 4 miles of trails give you plenty of other viewing opportunities. White-tailed deer, red foxes, and other small mammals might prove difficult to see, but turtles are often seen around the pond, even the threatened wood turtle.

Directions: *From U.S. Highway 206 in Bedminster, take County Route 512 west. Go 0.9 mile on CR 512 to Larger Cross Road. Turn left and proceed for 0.5 mile to the farm's driveway on the right.*

Ownership: Upper Raritan Watershed Association (908) 234-1852

Size: 150 acres   **Closest Town:** Bedminster

20. WILLOWWOOD ARBORETUM AND BAMBOO BROOK OUTDOOR EDUCATION CENTER

Description: Willowwood, named for a collection of 110 willows planted in the early 20th century, has about 3,500 species of native and exotic plants. Plantings blend in with untouched wild areas. Meadows, fields, and a forest on Western Hill border streams and the arboretum. Geologically, Willowwood is in the Piedmont Province, while Bamboo Brook lies in the Highlands Province. Both centers have 18th-century houses and Bamboo Brook has a formal garden designed by Martha Brookes Hutcheson.

Viewing Information: Foot trails start from the parking areas of both centers. Pick up a map at the Myers Visitor Center at Willowwood Arboretum. The trail through Long Meadow in Willowwood, to Bamboo Brook, gives you a chance to view many kinds of wildlife. Look for woodchucks, eastern blue-birds, and American goldfinches feeding in the fields. Northern harriers and red-tailed hawks are looking for the small rodents you might not see. Multitudes of songbirds migrate in spring and fall and nest in the woods and wetland areas. Down by the brook, look for wood frogs, southern leopard frogs, and crayfish. Tracks of red foxes, raccoons, white-tailed deer, and wild turkeys are more visible than the animals themselves.

Directions: *From the junction of U.S. Highway 206 and County Route 512, turn west onto CR 512 (Pottersville Road). Continue for 0.6 mile to Union Grove Road. Turn right and proceed 0.5 mile to Longview Road. Turn left on Longview Road. Entrances are 1 mile farther, on the left.*

Ownership: Morris County Park Commission (973) 326-7600

Size: Willowwood Arboretum 130 acres, Bamboo Brook Outdoor Education Center 100 acres

 **Closest Town:** Pottersville

Bluebirds prefer open, grassy areas, where they make their nests in wooden fence posts and hedgerow trees. Artificial nest boxes have helped them cope with the loss of many of these natural nesting sites.
SIMON B. LEVENTHAL

21. SPRUCE RUN AND ROUND VALLEY RECREATION AREAS

Description: Both recreation areas have reservoirs that attract large numbers of waterfowl on fall migration and during the winter. Spruce Run is next to Clinton Wildlife Management Area, which has more than 1,200 acres of fields and woodlands. Spruce Run and Round Valley offer wilderness campsites, available April 1 to October 31, for hikers and canoeists. Both have a variety of facilities and are very popular in the summer.

Viewing Information: Winter waterfowl watching is possible from many points around the reservoirs. Stop in at the offices for maps and information. The waterfowl most likely to be seen include mallards, American black ducks, canvasbacks, lesser scaup, ring-necked ducks, and Canada geese. ROUND VALLEY IS OPEN FOR HUNTING DURING PRESCRIBED SEASONS.

Directions: From Interstate 78, take exit 17 to New Jersey 31 north. Travel 3 miles to Van Syckel's Road. Turn left and travel 1.5 miles to the recreation area entrance on the left. For Round Valley, take I78 to exit 18. Take U.S. Highway 22 east 2.3 miles to recreation area signs. Follow signs to boat ramp and office.

Ownership: NJDEP Division of Parks and Forestry: Spruce Run (908)638-8572, Round Valley (908)236-6355

Size: Spruce Run 1,961 acres, Round Valley 3,639 acres

Closest Towns: Spruce Run: Clinton, Round Valley: Lebanon

New Jersey hosts two distinct populations of Canada geese: year-round residents and migratory geese, which pass through in the spring and fall.
TOM VEZO

22. SOUTH BRANCH RESERVATION–ECHO HILL ENVIRONMENTAL EDUCATION AREA

Description: The South Branch Reservation, almost 950 acres in size, was established to preserve the Raritan River and its environment. Evergreen bluffs, old farm fields, and the largest marsh in Hunterdon County are some of its preserved areas. The Echo Hill Environmental Education Area has a lodge with a conference room and restrooms; the former Stanton Station railroad station, now an activity center; and camping or cabins for groups. Prescott Brook flows through the site, which also has large sycamores in a river-bottom forest, mature spruce and pine plantations, and a manmade pond.

Viewing Information: A nature trail winds around the Echo Hill area, past the brook, through the evergreen forest, and through a second-growth hardwood forest. The conifer stands here are among New Jersey's best and support nesting Cooper's hawks, red-breasted nuthatches, and golden-crowned kinglets. Spring brings colorful wildflowers and migratory songbirds. In May and June, look for wood turtles, eastern box turtles, and snapping turtles. White-tailed deer may be encountered at any time. During the fall migration in September and October, you are sure to see some of those confusing fall warblers, a few waterfowl, and raptors. Owls and winter finches are part of the winter scene from November through March.

Directions: *Take New Jersey 31 south from Interstate 78/U.S. Highway 22 for 5 miles. Turn right onto Stanton Station Road and continue for 0.4 mile. Turn right at Lilac Drive, just before the railroad, and make a right turn at the entrance in another 0.4 mile.*

Ownership: Hunterdon County Park System (908) 782-1158

Size: 76 acres   **Closest Towns:** Stanton Station and Clinton

Saw-whet owls spend the day roosting in dense thickets, often close to the ground. At dusk, they become active and begin hunting for mice and other small animals. BRIAN P. BOWER

23. MUSCONETCONG RIVER RESERVATION, POINT MOUNTAIN SECTION

Description: Point Mountain, just south of the Musconetcong River, is one of the highest points in the region. It has a large expanse of maturing hardwood forest.

Viewing Information: A trail system of approximately 3 miles traverses this site, leading along the Musconetcong River and up to a lookout. The lookout is especially good in the fall for observing the small flights of hawks that occur in September and October. Some days, up to 200 birds use the updraft from the ridges on their flights south. More than 70 birds breed on the site, including the forest-interior species—ruffed grouse, pileated woodpeckers, acadian fly-catchers, and Kentucky and hooded warblers. May and June are the reservation's best birding months. Rare red-shouldered hawks and goshawks may also breed in this area.

Directions: *From New Jersey 31 in Hampton, take County Route 645 north and east along the Musconetcong River for about 4 miles. Turn right onto Point Mountain Road. Park at the left pullouts on either side of Point Mountain Road. Trailheads are near the bridge on Point Mountain Road and next to the Musconetcong River Reservation sign, near the junction of Point Mountain Road and CR 645.*

Ownership: Hunterdon County Park System (908) 782-1158

Size: 534 acres   **Closest Town:** Hampton

Listen for the drumming of the male ruffed grouse in the spring. Males "drum" from a low perch, usually a fallen log or tree stump, by beating their wings rapidly together. Drumming serves two purposes, to attract a mate and to defend territory. CHARLES H. WILLEY

METRO

The name "Metro" implies a heavily developed landscape, and, in many respects, it accurately describes large portions of this region. However, as you explore the area, a different picture emerges. From the cliffs of the Palisades, along the Hudson, to the wetlands of the Hackensack Meadowlands, to the gentle uplands of Union County, wildlife is everywhere.

As awareness of the importance of wildlife habitat has grown, the residents of the Metro region have rallied to maintain and enhance their remaining wild areas. Parks and natural areas have been connected to form "greenways," where bike and walking paths allow people to enjoy the outdoors while viewing the wildlife that also rely on these travelways.

Bordered on the east by the Hudson River and Raritan Bay, and on the west by the Highlands, the region contains a number of habitats, ranging from salty coves to upland forests. This diversity results in a vast array of wildlife—from harbor seals to the occasional black bear; and the area's wealth of bird life is simply extraordinary.

Although vast tracts of wetlands have been filled for development and landfills, large areas of estuarine habitat remain. These areas, the Hackensack Meadowlands and Liberty State Park among them, are critical nurseries for marine, as well as bird species. It surprises many to learn that within sight of the twin towers of the World Trade Center, sightings of snowy owls and peregrine falcons are not uncommon. These, and numerous other species, have adapted to life in the region, and countless other bird species use the meadows and other natural areas as stepping stones in their biannual migrations. The riparian corridors, greenways, and suburban parks also support a surprising variety of common mammals—raccoons, white-tailed deer, Virginia opossums, striped skunks, eastern cottontails, and woodchucks, as well as diverse populations of reptiles, amphibians, and breeding songbirds.

The effects of DDT wiped out the peregrine falcon in New Jersey by the 1960s. Thanks to an ambitious restoration project it now graces our skies once again. In fact, it can be seen near Newark and the Hudson River where several pairs nest on a building and the GW Bridge.
SIMON B. LEVENTHAL

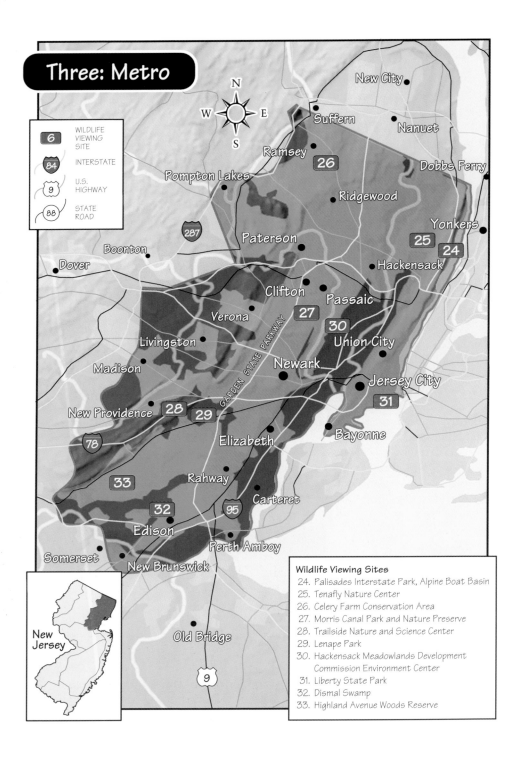

Three: Metro

Legend:
- **6** WILDLIFE VIEWING SITE
- **84** INTERSTATE
- **9** U.S. HIGHWAY
- **88** STATE ROAD

New City
Suffern
Nanuet
Ramsey
26
Dobbs Ferry
Pompton Lakes
Ridgewood
Yonkers
287
Paterson
25 **24**
Boonton
Hackensack
Dover
Clifton
Passaic
Verona
27
30
Livingston
Union City
Madison
Newark
Jersey City
New Providence
28 **29**
31
78
Elizabeth
Bayonne
33
Rahway
32
Carteret
95
Edison
Somerset
Perth Amboy
New Brunswick

GARDEN STATE PARKWAY

Old Bridge
9

New Jersey

Wildlife Viewing Sites
24. Palisades Interstate Park, Alpine Boat Basin
25. Tenafly Nature Center
26. Celery Farm Conservation Area
27. Morris Canal Park and Nature Preserve
28. Trailside Nature and Science Center
29. Lenape Park
30. Hackensack Meadowlands Development Commission Environment Center
31. Liberty State Park
32. Dismal Swamp
33. Highland Avenue Woods Reserve

MUSKRAT

PEREGRINE FALCON
WITH CHICKS

PALISADE
CLIFFS AND
HUDSON RIVER

WOOD RAT

OPOSSUM

BLUE HERON

PHRAGMITES

BLACK DUCK

PINTAIL DUCK

TUNDRA
SWAN

FIVE LINED SKINK

LADY'S
SLIPPER

WHITE PERCH

New York City forms an impressive backdrop for the Hackensack Meadowlands, a complex of brackish and freshwater marshes located in the most densely developed area on the east coast. These marshes provide a much-needed haven for wildlife in this urban setting. Ignored for many years as a wasteland, this area is now being protected and revitalized as a key link in the chain of migratory pathways stretching the length of New Jersey.

It is not uncommon in winter to see a snowy owl on the meadow or thousands of migrating waterfowl in tidal pools. Peregrine falcons nest on nearby inner-city bridges. Herons and egrets stalk the tidal creeks, looking for fish and frogs.

Description: The Palisades are the best remaining example of thick diabase in the United States. The cliffs formed approximately 190 million years ago, when magma from beneath the surface of the earth was forced upward between layers of sandstone and shale, making what is now known as diabase. The diabase, or trap rock, was quarried extensively in the last century, which led to the formation of the Park Commission to protect the Palisades from further destruction.

The Palisades Interstate Parkway is a scenic ride from the George Washington Bridge northward. Three lookouts offer spectacular views of the Palisades, the Hudson River, and the New York City skyline. Fort Lee Historic Park offers a glimpse into New Jersey's revolutionary past.

Viewing Information: The hiking trail from the parking area of the Alpine Boat Basin is an easy walk. Look for evidence of the last remaining eastern woodrat population in New Jersey. A native species, the woodrat is less aggressive than competing exotic rat species. The hiking trail from State Line Lookout down the cliff is a much more ambitious and challenging trail. Waterfowl seen on the river include Barrows goldeneyes, buffleheads, and canvasbacks in winter. View the fall migration of raptors from either the Alpine Boat Basin or State Line Lookout. The spring songbird migration is evident along the hiking trails. The Hudson River is a major spawning ground for shad, striped bass, and sturgeon.

Directions: *Take the Palisades Interstate Parkway north from Interstate 95 (last exit in New Jersey before the George Washington Bridge). Travel 7.5 miles to exit 2. Go east from exit 2 and downhill 1 mile to Henry Hudson Drive and the entrance to the Alpine Boat Basin, on left.*

Ownership: Palisades Interstate Park Commission (201) 768-1360

Size: 2,500 acres   **Closest Town:** Alpine

The last remaining population of eastern woodrats in New Jersey lives along the cliffs of the Palisades. These shy, timid little creatures are nocturnal and therefore not often seen. Frequently called "packrats" for their habit of collecting bright, shiny objects, they build stick and grass nests among the rocks in areas where rock slides have occurred. Mostly plant-eaters, they will occasionally eat insects. Look for piles of grass clippings as a telltale sign of their presence.

25. TENAFLY NATURE CENTER

Description: Tenafly Nature Center has a buttonbush swamp, streams, and a pond. The deciduous forest is mixed-oak, sugar maple, and black birch. Several trails allow the visitor to experience the diversity here. School groups are frequent visitors to the nature center. Many view with delight the eastern chipmunks that scurry in and around the interpretive center.

Viewing Information: Frogs and turtles are common in the spring and summer at Pfister's Pond, about 600 feet from the parking area on the main trail. Sunfish may be seen nesting in the pond at the trail's edge. Breeding birds that use the pond include wood ducks and green herons; black-crowned night herons and kingfishers are also present. For excellent songbird viewing, take the longer walks to the buttonbush swamp and through the woods in spring and fall. Trail maps are available at the interpretive center.

Directions: *From U.S. Highway 9W, take East Clinton Ave 1.9 miles west to Engle Street. Turn right and travel 0.7 mile to Hudson Ave. Turn right again and follow Hudson Avenue to its terminus.*

Ownership: Borough of Tenafly, managed by Tenafly Nature Center Association (201) 568-6093

Size: 52 acres   **Closest Town:** Tenafly

Green frogs are common and often found near shallow fresh water. Distinguished from the bullfrog by the two ridges that extend from the eye to the hind leg, they can often be seen near the edges of streams, ditches, and ponds. CLAY MYERS

METRO

26. CELERY FARM CONSERVATION AREA

Description: The Celery Farm is a delightful treasure—a small freshwater wetland with overgrown fields, hardwood swamp, uplands, and 20 acres of open water in the middle of suburban development. Birders report that 225 species of birds use this area throughout the year. Once drained and used to grow celery, the farm's elevated water levels now create several acres of flooded marsh. Dramatic numbers of nesting and migratory marsh birds arrive in spring and fall. Volunteers maintain an active nest box program for several species of cavity nesters. Parking is limited to ten cars.

Viewing Information: For an hour or two of birding, take a leisurely walk along the 1.3-mile footpath. The single loop trail around Lake Appert allows undisturbed viewing of wildlife. Red-winged blackbirds, yellow warblers, great egrets, double-crested cormorants, Canada geese, green herons, willow fly-catchers, Virginia rails, common moorhens, and soras are the most common birds along the trail. In the fall there are migrating swallows and hundreds of bobolinks.

Directions: *Take the Garden State Parkway exit 165 for Ridgewood Avenue west. Travel 0.8 mile to New Jersey 17 north. Travel north for 5.3 miles to the exit for Allendale. Follow East Allendale Avenue west for 1 mile to Franklin Turnpike. Turn right and go 0.3 mile to parking lot on right.*

Ownership: Allendale Borough (201) 327-3470

Size: 97 acres   **Closest Town:** Allendale

The streaked brown plumage of the American bittern allows it to blend into the background in the cattail and reed marshes where it spends most of its time. It will more likely be heard than seen in the spring since its "pump-er-lunk" call is loud and distinctive. CHARLES H. WILLEY

27. MORRIS CANAL PARK AND NATURE PRESERVE

Description: The Morris Canal Park is a bit of history and nature in the middle of a busy city. There are plenty of benches to stop and rest or reflect on as you walk. The trails wind through gardens and small stands of hardwood and mulberry trees. The canal and pond are stocked with fish.

Viewing Information: More than 25 species of birds have been viewed in the area. Mallards and domestic ducks are residents in both the canal and pond. Salamanders, frogs, turtles, and crayfish also live in the pond.

Directions: *From the Garden State Parkway north, go east on New Jersey 3. Take the Broad Street–Clifton exit and make a left at the light onto Broad Street. The Park is a short distance on the right, between Allwood Road and Van Houten Avenue.*

Ownership: City of Clifton (201) 473-5176

Size: 5 acres   **Closest Town:** Clifton

28. TRAILSIDE NATURE AND SCIENCE CENTER

Description: The center is located in a wooded preserve along the first and second Watchung Mountains. More than 13 miles of hiking trails are available. Facilities include a visitor center, museum, and planetarium. The visitor center is open from 1 P.M to 5 P.M. on most days; call ahead for information.

Viewing Information: White-tailed deer are abundant. Nature trails vary in length and provide good looks at many habitat types. The butterfly garden and backyard wildlife habitat are summer attractions. Wildlife can be viewed close-up from the visitor center parking lot during mulberry season from mid-June to July. Spring and fall migrations of warblers and hawks are visible from the parking lots and several trails.

Directions: *From US 22, take the Mountainside–New Providence Road exit. Proceed north (uphill) toward Mountainside on New Providence Road for 0.8 mile to Tracy Drive and turn right. At the traffic circle, take the third right (Summit Lane west) and proceed 0.6 mile to the center's parking area on your right.*

Ownership: Union County Division of Parks and Recreation (908) 789-3670

Size: 2,000 acres   **Closest Town:** Mountainside

29. LENAPE PARK

Description: Located in an urban setting, Lenape Park is on the floodplain of the north branch of the Rahway River and includes the Nomehegan and Black Brook tributaries. The habitats present in the park include hardwood uplands, floodplain forests, grassy fields, and wetlands. There is a pond at the park's west end that provides a resting and feeding area for migratory birds.

Viewing Information: Earthen berms parallel the waterways in the park and provide excellent viewing opportunities. There are good viewing opportunities in the parking lot, but an easy 1.5-mile walking trail is preferable; look for 100 species of birds, white-tailed deer, and a good variety of turtles. Spring migration brings 25 species of warblers, including blackburnian warblers. Summer nesting species include orchard and northern orioles and ruby-throated hummingbirds. Fall migration at the park brings sharp-shinned, broad-winged, and red-shouldered hawks, pied-billed grebes, common nighthawks, and several species of bat. Occasional visits by such birds as peregrine falcons, hooded mergansers, water pipits, and bobolinks keep bird watching interesting for all birders.

Directions: *From U.S. Highway 22 in Cranford, turn onto County Route 577 south which becomes County Route 509 east within 1 mile. Continue on CR 509 east for a short distance; the parking area is on your left (total distance from US 22 is less than 1 mile).*

Ownership: Union County Department of Parks and Recreation (908) 527-4900

Size: 387 acres   **Closest Towns:** Cranford, Westfield

A well-known summer resident, the ruby-throated hummingbird feeds entirely on nectar. It shows a preference for the color red. Some flowers, like the cardinal flower and trumpetvine with their long, slender throats, depend on the hummingbird for pollination. RAY DAVIS

30. HACKENSACK MEADOWLANDS DEVELOPMENT COMMISSION ENVIRONMENT CENTER

Description: The HMDC Environment Center sits in the center of the 110-acre Richard W. DeKorte Park, overlooking the Kingsland Tidal Impoundment. The adjoining Lyndhurst Nature Preserve is a landfill reclamation effort that turned an island of residential garbage into a lushly planted nature study area with spectacular vistas. Kingsland Overlook is also a landfill reclamation project with views of a tidal impoundment and the NYC skyline. Five plant and wildlife communities have been established within the project area: a wildflower meadow, butterfly meadow, eastern coastal grassland prairie, woody (shrub) field, and a young woodland and evergreen forest.

Viewing Information: More than 260 species of birds are attracted to the environment center's many habitats—from fresh and salt water wetlands to uplands. Each season has a predominant group of migrants. Residents include common moorhens, pied-billed grebes, ruddy ducks, and gadwalls. A variety of shorebirds pass through from July to September. Look for ospreys fishing in the impoundment. Blue, mud, and fiddler crabs, killifish, and northern diamondback terrapins inhabit the marsh. The Marsh Discovery Trail is part of a 1-mile loop around Kingsland tidal impoundment. Self-guided trails, seating, and observation areas are available for groups. Trail guides are available in the center or in boxes on bulletin boards near the parking lots. The center is closed on Sunday, but the trails remain open.

Directions: *From the New Jersey Turnpike, exit 16W, take New Jersey 3 west to NJ 17 south (Lyndhurst exit). Follow the ramp onto Polito Avenue and continue to the end. At the stop sign, turn left onto Valley Brook Avenue and continue 1.5 miles to its end. Continue straight across the railroad tracks to the environment center on the left.*

Ownership: Hackensack Meadowlands Development Commission (201) 460-1700; Environment Center (201) 460-8300

Size: 19,730 acres   **Closest Town:** Lyndhurst

Named for its long "ear" tufts, the long-eared owl is very secretive and seldom seen. By day it roosts in evergreen thickets and emerges at dusk to hunt in open meadows for small mammals.

NEW JERSEY DIVISION OF
FISH, GAME, AND WILDLIFE

31. LIBERTY STATE PARK

Description: Ferries travel to the Statue of Liberty and Ellis Island from the park and the New York City skyline looms large in the background. At the edge of an industrial park center overlooking the Upper Bay of the Hudson river, the state park has a natural area and nature center. Liberty Walk is a great place to view the birds in the bay.

Viewing Information: Because it contains both estuarine and upland habitats, the park's list of resident birds currently numbers 210. From the information center, walk out to the piers, the overlook, and along Liberty Walk. On a windy day this can be quite a challenge. During the summer, herons and egrets nesting in the Arthur Kill regularly feed in the salt marsh. During fall migration, the fairly shallow waters between the park and Ellis Island attract numerous waterfowl. Visit the interpretive center, north of the information center, on Freedom Way. Long-eared owls are often seen in winter near the center. A variety of gulls and ducks frequent the salt marsh between the center and the walkway. During spring, migrating shorebirds line the waterfront.

Directions: Liberty State Park is most easily accessed from the New Jersey Turnpike Extension, exit 14 B. It is 1 mile from the turnpike toll booth to the information center. The road is called Morris Pesin Drive, but you may not see the road sign. Follow the signs to the state park.

Ownership: NJDEP Division of Parks and Forestry (201) 915-3409

Size: 36 acres   **Closest Town:** Jersey City

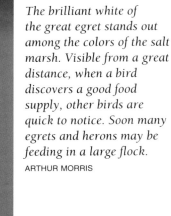

The brilliant white of the great egret stands out among the colors of the salt marsh. Visible from a great distance, when a bird discovers a good food supply, other birds are quick to notice. Soon many egrets and herons may be feeding in a large flock.
ARTHUR MORRIS

32. DISMAL SWAMP

Description: Dismal Swamp is one of the last remaining wetlands in a highly urbanized environment. It is designated a "priority wetland" by the U.S. Fish & Wildlife Service. The area features wetlands that are of unique ecological value, upland deciduous forests with mature trees more than 50 years old, and abandoned fields rich with herbaceous vegetation. The open swampland along Bound Brook provides a floodwater storage buffer for surrounding developments.

Viewing Information: Take the Dismal Swamp Trail from Metuchen for a short but interesting hike through a portion of the swamp. The trail is fun for children and unique in that it uses fallen trees as observation blinds and bridges. The swamp supports a variety of wildlife—sightings of at least 165 bird species are recorded each year. Look for green herons, American bitterns, American black ducks, northern harriers, Virginia rails, spotted sandpipers, yellow-billed cuckoos, and eastern phoebes in the wetlands and fields. Songbirds are numerous in the wetland and upland forests and endangered loggerhead shrikes are reported to breed here. Sightings of endangered grasshopper sparrows are also on record. The swamp's mammals include white-tailed deer, raccoons, eastern cottontails, and red foxes. Eastern box turtles, spotted turtles, black racers, and northern water snakes are among the reptiles present.

Directions: *From New Jersey 27 in Metuchen, turn north onto Central Avenue and go left (west) to Liberty Street (note sign for Liberty Corporate Center). Proceed for 0.6 mile to a cul-de-sac. The entrance to the observation trail is located near the Green Acres sign. There is no parking at the larger Edison portion of the swamp. However, Talmadge Road (from NJ 27) crosses the swamp and provides an elevated view.*

Ownership: Edison Township, Borough of Metuchen (908) 632-8520

Size: 240 acres in Edison, almost 10 acres in Metuchen

Closest Towns: Edison and Metuchen

Small islands of undeveloped land in highly urbanized areas provide critical habitat for wildlife. These gems are used as feeding and resting sites during migration, act as travelways, and provide important nesting habitat for wildlife that has adapted to life among urban sprawl.

33. HIGHLAND AVENUE WOODS RESERVE

Description: This is an urban preserve, with streams, woods, and fields, situated between industrial and residential development. Habitat types include several upland communities and two wetlands communities, which provide breeding, resting, and feeding areas for a variety of wildlife.

Viewing Information: Take the trails from the Sylvania Place road access. People who bird at the reserve record about 40 resident and migrant species. Loggerhead shrikes, a state endangered species, are seen along the stream, as are black-crowned night herons. Look for red-tailed hawks, ruby-throated hummingbirds, and wood thrushes in the spring and summer. Black-throated green warblers, warbling vireos, and yellow-rumped warblers are seen in spring. Red-backed salamanders, northern spring peepers, and wood frogs are among the denizens of the wetlands. Mammal signs are present, including raccoon tracks and muskrat holes, and you are sure to catch sight of a gray squirrel. A variety of butterflies enjoy the flowering plants in the reserve.

Directions: *From Interstate 287, take the Edison exit from the north or the Durham Avenue exit from the south. From Durham Avenue, turn left onto Hamilton Boulevard, then right onto South Clinton Avenue, then right onto Sylvania Place. From the Edison exit, turn left onto Stelton Avenue, then right onto Hamilton Boulevard and proceed as above.*

Ownership: Borough of South Plainfield (908) 226-9000

Size: Approximately 25 acres   **Closest Town:** South Plainfield

Monarch butterflies are unique in that they migrate to Mexico for the winter and return to the United States in spring to mate and die. BRECK P. KENT

PIEDMONT REGION

The Piedmont Region is part of the Triassic Lowland Physiographic Province extending from the Blue Ridge Mountains in the south to Connecticut in the north. The landscape of this region is gently rolling lowland dissected by broad, winding river valleys with well-developed floodplains. The gentle contours of the countryside are interrupted by a number of distinctly higher, rocky ridges and hills, including the Hunterdon Plateau and Sourland Mountain. These landforms were created during the breakup of the Pangean "supercontinent" approximately 200 million years ago as rift valleys formed, filled, eroded, tilted, uplifted, became injected with magma, and eroded further. Today, the land continues to be shaped through weathering and erosion.

Although the heavily developed U.S. Route 1 corridor bisects this region, it is still dominated largely by farm fields, pastures, woodlands, swamps, and rocky ridges. Fortunately, many acres within this area are preserved as public open space. The Hunterdon County Park System, Washington Crossing State Park, Assunpink Wildlife Management Area, Bull's Island Recreation Area, and the Stony Brook–Millstone Watershed Association are some of the public lands that offer high quality wildlife-watching opportunities.

In early spring, the forest floor is lined with lycopodium and skunk cabbage. As spring progresses, May apples, violets, jack-in-the-pulpits, wild azaleas, sweetgum, hickory, tulip-poplar, black cherry, and beech trees bloom. Greenbrier, Virginia creeper, poison ivy, and wild grape creep over the underbrush. In the wooded bogs and swamps of the region, red maple, black gum,

ash, and birch are the dominant trees, while blueberry, sweet pepperbush, and buttonbush grow in the understory. Sphagnum moss, swamp rose, and blue flag iris provide a herbaceous layer.

Woodpeckers, blue jays, northern cardinals, tufted titmice, and chickadees are glimpsed here year-round. During spring and fall, the forest is abuzz with the songs of migrant birds. In winter, mink tracks are a common sight along the banks of streams. Listen and look for several species of amphibian, especially during the spring breeding season. Eastern chipmunks, gray squirrels, and white-tailed deer are the most commonly seen mammals. Look for waterfowl, particularly wood ducks, in the rivers and streams.

A woodland bird preferring deciduous woods, the tufted titmouse is omnivorous, eating insects and fruit. A small curious bird, it is easy to call in. Look for titmice flitting around from branch to branch.
LEONARD LEE RUE III

Although its size is decreasing at an alarming rate, this region still supports large areas of agricultural land. Both hay fields and fields lying fallow are important because they provide prime habitat for endangered grassland birds, including upland sandpipers, vesper sparrows, grasshopper sparrows, and bobolinks, as well as mammals, including coyotes, white-tailed deer, and eastern cottontail rabbits. Watch for red-tailed hawks and American kestrels hunting over open fields or perching in a tree or on a telephone wire. Wild turkeys also frequent open fields and meadows.

Ground-nesting killdeer feed in open areas, while swallows feed on insects overhead. In the fall, thousands of Canada geese feed on cut grain, and sandpipers, dowitchers, and yellowlegs search puddles after autumn rains. Field edges contain a mix of native and ornamental shrubs and understory trees such as sassafras, dogwood, Russian olive, multiflora rose, and blackberry brambles, which provide food and cover for wildlife. Edge habitats are particularly attractive to northern mockingbirds, woodchucks, bobwhite quail, and ring-necked pheasants.

At higher elevations, the vegetation reflects the drier habitat and thinner soil. Oak-hickory forests are bursting with grasses, forbes, mosses, and lichens found growing on exposed south and west facing slopes. Toads, eastern box turtles, eastern chipmunks, gray squirrels, songbirds, and white-tailed deer are the main inhabitants of this dry, less-diverse habitat.

Preceding page: *Fall is a wonderful time for wildlife viewing in the Piedmont. At this time of year wildlife populations are at their highest level, but if you don't see many animals, you can still enjoy the splendid display of color.* DAVID LOVELESS

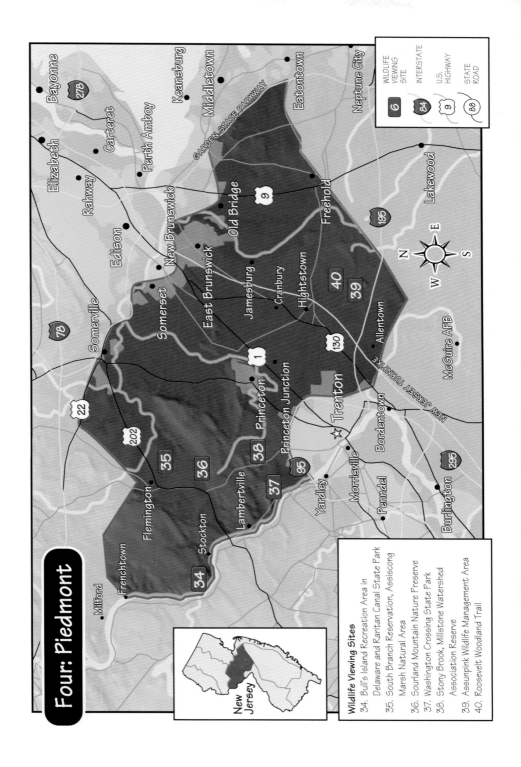

Four: Piedmont

Wildlife Viewing Sites

34. Bull's Island Recreation Area in Delaware and Raritan Canal State Park
35. South Branch Reservation, Assiscong Marsh Natural Area
36. Sourland Mountain Nature Preserve
37. Washington Crossing State Park
38. Story Brook, Millstone Watershed Association Reserve
39. Assunpink Wildlife Management Area
40. Roosevelt Woodland Trail

Legend

- 6 — WILDLIFE VIEWING SITE
- 84 — INTERSTATE
- 9 — U.S. HIGHWAY
- 88 — STATE ROAD

New Jersey

GOLDFINCH

EASTERN MEADOWLARK

SHAD FISHING

UPLAND SANDPIPER

PHEASANTS

SKUNK

MILK SNAKE

The Piedmont is characterized by low, rolling hills and well-drained, fertile soil. Farm fields, especially those not in crop rotation, provide important habitat for many edge-dwelling species. Many animals visit fields at different times of the day or year to meet a variety of needs. Fields are generally very different from surrounding habitats. They heat more quickly than other areas due to their constant exposure to sunlight.

TIGER SWALLOWTAIL

EASTERN BLUEBIRD

BARN SWALLOW

GRAY SQUIRREL

DOWNY WOODPECKER

WHITE-TAILED DEER

RED FOX

Jane Eyre '96

VOLE

EASTERN COTTONTAIL

White-tailed deer come to fields to browse on fresh green shoots in the spring. Hibernators like woodchucks and snakes come out to bask in the sun. Flowering plants draw insects, which attract birds and later produce seeds, which are eaten by birds and rodents. The loose soil attracts burrowers—toads and meadow voles, for instance, which, in turn, attract red foxes, hawks, and owls. Fields also provide cover for ground-nesting birds and small mammals, including eastern cottontails.

34. BULL'S ISLAND RECREATION AREA IN DELAWARE AND RARITAN CANAL STATE PARK

Description: Once a tow path for the historic Delaware & Raritan Canal, the linear D & R Canal State Park is now a popular recreation corridor for canoeing, hiking, and bicycling. Bull's Island Recreation Area has a 39-acre natural area protecting rare species habitat. The pedestrian bridge over the Delaware River at Bull's Island provides birders with a rare opportunity to look up into the trees bordering the river. The Griggstown site has a museum with exhibits and artifacts relating to the history of the canal.

Viewing Information: Bull's Island is one of the few New Jersey nesting sites for northern parula warblers, cerulean warblers, yellow-throated warblers, and acadian flycatchers. Walk through the Natural Area on a trail beginning near the office. The trail parallels the canal and allows you to view the canal and river.

Directions: *From U.S. Highway 202 just above Lambertville, take New Jersey 29 north for 5.5 miles to the entrance of Bull's Island. To get to the Griggstown Causeway, take U. S. Highway 1 north of Princeton to County Route 632. Follow CR 632 through Kendall Park for 4.4 miles to a T intersection with Canal Road. Turn left and travel 0.6 mile to the causeway on the right.*

Ownership: NJDEP Division of Parks and Forestry (609) 397-2949

Size: Bull's Island 79 acres, D & R Canal State Park 3,578 acres

Closest Towns: Stockton and Kendall Park

The prothonotary warbler is the only eastern warbler to nest in tree cavities. Preferring damp, swampy river bottoms and wooded stream corridors, this colorful warbler feeds on insects on fallen trees near the water's surface.
DR. PETER J. LEKOS

35. SOUTH BRANCH RESERVATION–ASSISCONG MARSH NATURAL AREA

Description: The largest herbaceous wetland in the county is less than a mile from busy New Jersey 31. The marsh vegetation is composed primarily of bulrushes, but there are also small stands of pin oak–red maple forest and buttonbush shrubs.

Viewing Information: Park in the small lot and walk north along the road next to the river, or look from your car as you drive slowly along the road. Birds and mammals use the bulrushes for food and nesting cover. Look for woodchucks, muskrats, Canada geese, rails, wood ducks, and common yellowthroats. Great blue herons, ospreys, and belted kingfishers frequently fish the waters. Look for waterfowl from February to May and September to November.

Directions: *From Flemington, take New Jersey 31 north to County Route 612 (Bartles Corner Road). Turn right and travel 0.7 mile to River Road. Turn left and go 0.1 mile to parking area.*

Ownership: Hunterdon County Park System (908) 782-1158

Size: 24 acres   **Closest Town:** Flemington

36. SOURLAND MOUNTAIN NATURE PRESERVE

Description: Heavily forested Sourland Mountain stands amid cultivated fields interspersed with housing developments. It is a forested gem amidst the farmland of central New Jersey.

Viewing Information: From the parking area, explore Sourland Mountain from several unmarked hiking trails. Spring migration is an excellent time to look in the upland and wetland forests for neotropical songbirds. Spring wildflowers are abundant, too. Look for plenty of reptiles and amphibians in the summer.

Directions: *From New Jersey 31/U. S. Highway 202 at Ringoes, go east on County Route 602 (Wertsville Road) for 3.5 miles. Turn right (south) onto County Route 607 and travel up the mountain. Turn left in 1.8 miles and go straight into the parking area, not left or right into the driveways of neighboring private residences.*

Ownership: Hunterdon County Park System (908) 782-1158

Size: 273 acres   **Closest Town:** Ringoes

37. WASHINGTON CROSSING STATE PARK

Description: The American Revolution is commemorated here by the Trenton Battle Monument, but the area is best known for General Washington's famed crossing of the Delaware River on Christmas night, 1776. The historic Ferry House, where Washington's army was assembled before the crossing, provides another attraction for visitors. The woodlands of the park are successional mixed-oak forests, which include southern red, white, and black oaks.

Viewing Information: Follow the well-marked roads to the nature center and a system of trails that varies in length from 0.25 to 1 mile. The trails offer easy 20 to 40-minute walks. The wildlife observation blind is 10 minutes away and overlooks a stream. Pick up a trail map at the nature center. The park has white-tailed deer, gray squirrels, and eastern chipmunks, as well as eastern cottontails, raccoons, and many birds. Listen and look for mallards, blue jays, red-bellied woodpeckers, eastern (rufous-sided) towhees, and American crows.

Directions: *From Exit 1 on Interstate 95, take New Jersey 29 south for 2.8 miles. Turn onto Washington Crossing–Pennington Road and travel 0.7 mile to park entrance.*

Ownership: NJDEP Division of Parks and Forestry (609) 737-0623

Size: 841 acres   **Closest Town:** Titusville

38. STONY BROOK–MILLSTONE WATERSHED ASSOCIATION RESERVE

Description: The Stony Brook–Millstone Watershed Association's mission is to improve the quality of the natural environment in the area drained by the two rivers. The association addresses issues such as stream corridor protection and watershed management, and also maintains a nature reserve and an organic farm. Buttinger Nature Center offers programs and exhibits.

Viewing Information: The reserve's six trails provide 8 miles of walking through grassy fields, forests, wetlands, and around a pond. Pick up a trail map, guide, and wildlife checklist, which expound the mammals, birds, reptiles, and amphibians that frequent the area. Look for invertebrates at the pond. Common mammals include white-tailed deer, red and gray squirrels, red foxes, woodchucks, white-footed mice, eastern cottontails, and muskrats.

Directions: *From New Jersey 31, north of Pennington, turn right (east) onto Titus Mill Road. Continue on Titus Mill Road for 1.2 miles to the reserve entrance, marked by a sign saying Watershed Nature Center.*

Ownership: Stony Brook–Millstone Watershed Association (609) 737-7592

Size: 535 acres   **Closest Town:** Pennington

39. ASSUNPINK WILDLIFE MANAGEMENT AREA

Description: The three lakes at Assunpink are popular rest stops for migrating waterfowl in the fall. Adjacent to large areas of fields and hedgerows, Assunpink is one of the best birding areas in central New Jersey.

Viewing Information: Pull into any of the grassy parking areas near the office. In the spring and summer, these fields are home to grassland bird species, including grasshopper sparrows and vesper sparrows. Throughout the year, hawks fly over, and owls come out at dusk and dawn. White-tailed deer and red foxes are plentiful and northern harriers cruise the fields for smaller mammals. Assunpink and Stone Tavern lakes contain largemouth bass, chain pickerel, and pumpkinseed, and are popular with Canada geese and a variety of ducks during their fall migration. These lakes also attract osprey, which like to fish here during migration. Drive along the road that parallels Assunpink Lake, the largest on the tract, for good views of waterfowl.

Assunpink WMA is a natural area with no facilities. OPEN FOR HUNTING DURING PRESCRIBED SEASONS.

Directions: *From Interstate 195, take exit 11. Go north on Imlaystown Road for 1.2 miles. Turn right onto Clarksburg–Robbinsville Road at second crossroads (no roadsigns) and proceed for 1.5 miles to the WMA office. Maps and information are available at the office.*

Ownership: NJDEP, Division of Fish, Game, and Wildlife (609) 259-2132

Size: 5,664 acres   **Closest Towns:** Roosevelt, Clarksburg, and Hightstown

PIEDMONT

The eastern cottontail is an "edge" species, thriving in border areas, hedgerows, weedy growth, dense high grass, and shrubby thickets.
LEN RUE, JR.

Description: Roosevelt is a small, planned community, dating from the early 20th century, but all around it suburbs are taking over. The trail through the hamlet is on the flood plain of Empty Box Brook, which flows through one of the last intact forest plots in the area. The woodland site is at least 50 years old, and is a South Jersey beech-oak upland forest.

Viewing Information: During the spring and summer, a profusion of wildflowers takes over the marsh and bog surrounding the stream; the blooms of dwarf ginseng, pinxterflower, and cardinal flowers are tremendous. The bogs contain shrubs more typical of habitats farther south—buttonbush and sweet pepperbush. Wildlife watchers should look and listen for gray tree frogs and wood frogs in the marsh. Minks, raccoons, and white-tailed deer are common. Three owl species are often seen, in addition to many forest songbirds. On a water tower north of town, both turkey and black vultures roost in the winter.

Directions: From Interstate 195, take exit 8 north onto County Route 539. Continue on CR 539 for about 4 miles to Windsor Road. Turn right onto Windsor Road and continue eastward for almost 3 miles. Turn right (south) onto County Route 571 and follow it 1.5 miles into Roosevelt. At the municipal building, take a right turn onto Pine Drive and travel 0.5 mile to its end.

Ownership: Borough of Roosevelt (609) 448-0539

Size: about 25 acres   **Closest Town:** Roosevelt

Raccoons prefer to live in wooded areas with water nearby. They are very adaptable creatures that will eat whatever is available: berries, nuts, frogs, eggs, snails, crayfish, even small rodents. They will use dens on the ground or in a tree.
BRECK P. KENT

COASTAL REGION

Forming a ribbonlike border along New Jersey's eastern edge, the Coastal Region consists of barrier islands; broad, shallow bogs; tidal salt marshes; and upland edges. Of all the landscapes in New Jersey, this region's is the most dynamic. Its contours change noticeably from year to year and even from one day to the next. From the bleak harshness of the beach to the tangled lushness of

mixed-hardwood uplands, the coast is teeming with wildlife and unique plant communities.

New Jersey's coast supports hundreds of species of fish, turtles, and marine mammals. Whales and dolphins are common sights offshore. Gulls, plovers, and sanderlings search for tasty morsels where the water meets the sandy beach. Least terns, black skimmers, and piping plovers, some of New Jersey's most endangered birds, are able to coexist with people thanks to the help of dedicated biologists, volunteers, and cooperative shore communities.

On the dunes, just behind the beaches, the vegetation is characteristically low-growing and consists of dunegrass, sea rocket, beach pea, cocklebur, and seaside goldenrod. Meadow voles, white-footed mice, and eastern cottontails are common enough to be prey for red and gray foxes. Skunks, raccoons, and opossums populate the thickets and forests between and behind the dunes.

Dominant tree species include American holly, black cherry, Spanish oak, white oak, blackjack oak, and red cedar. Beach plum, bayberry, juneberry, blueberry, catbrier, and Japanese honeysuckle make up the shrub layer.

Fowler's toads, one of only a few species of coastal amphibians, frequent the rainwater pools between the dunes, where they are fed upon by garter, king, and hognose snakes. Other coastal reptiles include fence lizards and eastern box turtles in the upland and northern diamond-backed terrapins, mud turtles, and snapping turtles in the marshes and dune ponds.

New Jersey's coastline forms the eastern boundary of the Atlantic flyway, the migratory pathway used by birds migrating along the eastern seaboard. During migration, large concentrations of migrating songbirds and raptors crowd the shrub thickets, dune woodlands, and wooded upland edges of

New Jersey's artificial reefs provide shelter for many ocean dwelling creatures, including the northern lobster, who hides among the many cracks and crevices. HERB SEGARS

marshes. Tidal marshes, sand dunes, coastal forests, and mixed-hardwood uplands are home to a variety of wildlife: white-tailed deer, muskrat, otter, raccoon, red and gray foxes, reptiles, and insects. The extensive salt marsh ecosystem supports an amazing variety of breeding herons, egrets, wading birds, terns, gulls, and an increasing osprey population.

Human impact on the coastal landscape is becoming more severe as development replaces the dunes and barrier islands. Due to ever-increasing human encroachment, most coastal landscapes are able to support wildlife populations in only small, fragmented reserves. Two notable exceptions are

Preceding page: *Salt marsh tide pools are important feeding areas for many species of wildlife. Killifishes and mummichogs are abundant and feed heavily on mosquite larvae. In turn, herons, egrets, and raccoons feed on the minnows. Dabbling ducks feed on the plant seeds found along the pool edges.* DWIGHT HISCANO

Island Beach State Park and Sandy Hook, part of the Gateway National Recreation Area. Island Beach, with its extensive vegetated dune system and dune forest, is a prime example of how the barrier islands in New Jersey looked before development.

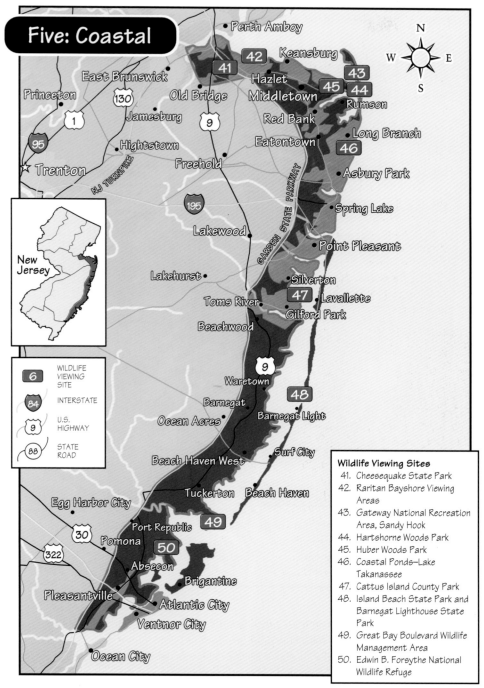

Five: Coastal

New Jersey

WILDLIFE VIEWING SITE 6
INTERSTATE 84
U.S. HIGHWAY 9
STATE ROAD 88

Wildlife Viewing Sites
41. Cheesequake State Park
42. Raritan Bayshore Viewing Areas
43. Gateway National Recreation Area, Sandy Hook
44. Hartshorne Woods Park
45. Huber Woods Park
46. Coastal Ponds—Lake Takanassee
47. Cattus Island County Park
48. Island Beach State Park and Barnegat Lighthouse State Park
49. Great Bay Boulevard Wildlife Management Area
50. Edwin B. Forsythe National Wildlife Refuge

BLUEFISH

CANVASBACK

HARLEQUIN

OLD SQUAW

SNOW GOOSE

REDHEAD

BRANDT

LAUGHING GULLS

BLACK SKIMMER

MOLE CRAB

SANDERLINGS

BLUE CRAB

ATLANTIC SURF CLAM

The Coastal Region is New Jersey's most diverse ecosystem. In summer, just offshore, bottlenosed dolphins frolic in the waves. Gulls, plovers, and sanderlings search for tasty morsels at the surf line; black skimmers and common terns dive for small fish offshore. Common terns have a nesting colony on the beach at Barnegat Light. Large concentrations of songbirds and raptors crowd the shrub thickets and

LITTLE SKATE

OSPREY

BOTTLENOSED DOLPHIN

SEASIDE GOLDENROD

COMMON TERN

GHOST CRAB

DUNE GRASS

COQUINAS

BAYBERRY

SKATE CASE

HOLLY

dune woodlands during migration. Waterfowl are common in the back bays and
tidal marshes in winter. Marine life abounds along the ocean beaches and in the
tidal creeks and back bays. Mole crabs and coquina live in the turbulent zone
where water meets beach, moving up and down the beach with the tide.

41. CHEESEQUAKE STATE PARK

Description: Cheesequake, one of the more accessible state parks, is located in the transition zone between northern and southern vegetation: it has open fields, salt and freshwater marshes, an Atlantic white cedar swamp, a small pine barrens, and a stand of northeastern hardwood forest. The Interpretive Center is an easy walk down a short trail. Displays, exhibits, and regular programs come alive with some captive critters.

Viewing Information: Mammals in the woods include gray squirrels, eastern chipmunks, raccoons, striped skunks, red and gray foxes, and an occasional white-tailed deer. More than 186 species of birds have been sighted at the park, so pick up a bird checklist. Birds to look for in the marsh include great blue herons, nesting ospreys, northern harriers, and rails. There are muskrats and northern diamond-backed terrapins in the marshes. Blue crabs are found during late summer in Hook's Creek. The longest trail takes about 90 minutes to walk and takes you over various terrain and through many habitats. Trail guides are available at the center or park office. For a spectacular view of pink lady's slipper take the Yellow Trail in spring.

Directions: *From exit 120 on the Garden State Parkway, turn right on Matawan Road. Travel 0.5 mile to Morristown Road. Turn right and go 0.7 mile to Gordon Avenue. Turn right and go 1 mile into the park.*

Ownership: NJDEP Division of Parks and Forestry (732) 566-2161

Size: 1,274 acres   **Closest Town:** Cheesequake

Although secretive, red foxes are common. Often tracks and scat are the only signs you will see. They frequent areas with both fields and woods and often rest during the day on a slight rise from which they can view the surrounding area.
HERB SEGARS

42. RARITAN BAYSHORE VIEWING AREAS

The viewing areas along Raritan Bay are close to each other and combine to give an overall look at Raritan Bay wildlife, as well as a glimpse of the New York City skyline. The bayfront is an important waterfowl feeding area. Salt marsh views are particularly rewarding at the extreme eastern and western ends of Port Monmouth Road in the town of Port Monmouth. View the marsh from your car, or take a walk from any of the waterfront parking areas. From New Jersey 36, take Main Street in Belford (Port Monmouth's neighbor to the east) to Port Monmouth Road.

RARITAN RIVERFRONT

Description: This is a large parking area next to the highway with a marvelous view of Raritan Bay.

Viewing Information: A few steps from your car puts you on a small boardwalk and fishing pier, providing a great panoramic view of Raritan Bay. Travel a few steps more to take a stroll along the beach. The bay is important for migrating waterfowl, so the best time to visit is in the fall. However, if you visit in winter, bring a spotting scope to view rafts of ducks on the bay.

Directions: From New Jersey 35 in Laurence Harbor, turn north onto Laurence Parkway, which leads to the parking area on the bay.

Ownership: Laurence Harbor, Old Bridge Township

Size: Less than 1 acre **Closest Town:** Laurence Harbor, Old Bridge Township

TREASURE LAKE

Description: Treasure Lake is a small freshwater lake bounded by a residential community on its landward side and by dune cliffs and a seawall bordering Raritan Bay. Marshes surround much of the lake.

Viewing Information: Trails meander through the wooded southeastern section of the lake and lead to the seawall. From the mini-parking lot at the end of Woodland Drive, trails access the top of the seawall for a view of Raritan Bay or, in the opposite direction, the lakeshore. From the Lakeshore Drive parking lot the walk is about 0.25 mile.

Directions: From New Jersey 35 in the middle of Cliffwood Beach, take Cliffwood Avenue east for 0.5 mile. Bear left when Cliffwood Avenue ends at the intersection of West Concourse and South Concourse. Take the first right, onto North Concourse. Turn left in 0.2 mile onto Woodland Drive. To get to the larger parking lot on Lakeshore Drive, take Cliffwood Avenue for 0.5 mile. Bear left at West and South Concourse roads and continue on Greenwood Avenue. In 0.4 mile, turn right onto Lakeshore Drive and continue 0.2 mile to beachfront parking lot on the right.

Ownership: Aberdeen Township (732) 583-4200

Size: 34 acres **Closest Town:** Cliffwood Beach, Aberdeen Township

43. GATEWAY NATIONAL RECREATION AREA, SANDY HOOK

Description: Sandy Hook is a long slender peninsula that stretches almost 6.5 miles into the New York City Harbor. The park includes salt marshes, hiking trails, and habitat for migratory shorebirds. Nature and history programs are offered throughout the year. Sandy Hook is extremely popular on summer weekends, so plan on arriving early or late in the day to avoid temporary closures due to traffic congestion.

Viewing Information: Sandy Hook Bay is a popular place for viewing a variety of wildlife. The Audubon Society provides a sighting list, available at the Spermaciti Cove Visitor Center, along with maps and trail guides. Observe the osprey nesting platform from the boardwalk across from the visitor center or the numerous ducks that inhabit the bay waters of Sandy Hook. The great blue herons, green herons, and egrets at Horseshoe Cove Salt Marsh make Plum Island a great place for birding, and the North Pond Observation Deck is an ideal spot to watch the spring and fall hawk migrations. The South Beach Dune Trail is an excellent place to find songbirds and warblers in the spring. The winter beaches have scores of snow buntings and herring, great black-backed, and ring-billed gulls.

Directions: *From the Garden State Parkway exits 117 from the north or 105 from the south, follow New Jersey 36 for approximately 12 miles directly into the Recreation Area. The visitor center is 2 miles from the entrance.*

Ownership: U.S. National Park Service (732) 872-5900

Size: 1,665 acres   **Closest Towns:** Highlands, Sea Bright

At black skimmer nesting colonies you will often see signs and fencing meant to protect the birds from disturbances that will expose the eggs or chicks to the elements and predators. Please enjoy the birds from a distance. CLAY MYERS

44. HARTSHORNE WOODS PARK

Description: This forest provides a unique combination of oak, American sycamore, and tulip-poplar, along with a remnant of the once-plentiful maritime holly forest. From high on Rocky Point, there is also an incredible view overlooking the Navesink and Shrewsbury tidal rivers, the barrier island, and Sandy Hook, all the way to the Atlantic Ocean.

Viewing Information: Birding is splendid here. Ospreys, belted kingfishers, bank swallows, and egrets feed in and over the waters in the summer. Ducks winter in the rivers, and the fall and spring warbler migrations are a treat. Trail maps are available at the kiosk next to the parking area. Viewing areas to seek out include Rocky Point, a mile-long walk, and Blackfish Cove, which is off the 1.5-mile loop trail. The trails are moderate to steep and mostly paved.

Directions: From New Jersey 36 in Highlands, turn right on Navesink Avenue and proceed to park less than 0.5 mile on left.

Ownership: Monmouth County Park System (732) 842-4000

Size: 736 acres   **Closest Town:** Highlands

45. HUBER WOODS PARK

Description: In 1974, the farm and home at Huber Woods were donated to Monmouth County and transformed into a park. The farmhouse and outbuildings now serve as an environmental center and reptile house, respectively. Set in mixed suburban and rural surroundings, the farm's oak-hickory woods and pastureland overlook the Navesink River, and 6 miles of trails let you walk, hike, bike, or ride through a meadow, tulip poplar grove, and oak woods. The environmental center, just uphill from the park system's Equestrian Program Center, is a local information source for the New Jersey Coastal Heritage Trail.

Viewing Information: For an easy walk, take the Nature Loop, a short path that highlights the diversity of the woods. Vine-covered thickets offer food and shelter to songbirds and eastern cottontails. In the fall, look for migrating birds and butterflies. Native plants that attract wildlife are a highlight of the Discovery Path, a quarter-mile long barrier-free trail south of the environmental center. A guide is available at the center. Small aquatic animals live in the pond and wildflowers bloom with butterflies in the summer.

Directions: From New Jersey 35 in Middletown, travel east on Navesink River Road, just north of the Cooper Avenue Bridge, for 2.8 miles to Brown's Dock Road and turn left (north). Park entrance is at the top of the hill.

Ownership: Monmouth County Park System (732) 872-2670

Size: 258 acres   **Closest Town:** Navesink

46. COASTAL PONDS–LAKE TAKANASSEE

Description: This string of coastal ponds from Monmouth University east to the ocean is located in a suburban area. Lake Takanassee is the largest and closest to the ocean, but also look for more coastal ponds southward along the Jersey shore from Long Branch to the Manasquan Inlet.

Viewing Information: All of the coastal ponds can be viewed from your car. Quiet, residential streets with low speed limits let you meander around the ponds at your leisure. If you do park your car on the street, a walk of 20 feet takes you to the edge of any of the ponds. Wintering gulls and waterfowl use the freshwater ponds for feeding and resting. Each pond seems to attract its own species: canvasbacks may be in one, while Barrows goldeneyes may be found in another. Park your car and walk across the highway at any crosswalk to scan the ocean. Scoters and gannets are often seen off the coast.

Directions: From New Jersey 36 in Long Branch, travel south on County Route 57 (Ocean Avenue) for 2.5 miles. Turn right onto North Lake Drive. For access to the west ponds, travel north from North Lake Drive on CR 57 to NJ 25 (Cedar Avenue). Turn left and take any of the roads on your left (south). Parking is along the road.

Ownership: City of Long Branch and Monmouth University (732) USA-BIRD

Size: About 10 acres **Closest Towns:** Long Branch, West Long Branch

The most common wild duck in the northern hemisphere, the mallard population in North America is estimated at nine million. Hardy and adaptable, mallards can be seen on almost any shallow body of fresh water. A. AND E. MORRIS

47. CATTUS ISLAND COUNTY PARK

Description: Cattus Island is actually a peninsula between Silver Bay and Barnegat Bay. The park contains more than 200 acres of tidal salt marsh, 100 acres of freshwater wetlands, and more than 100 acres of upland forest. It is an ecological gem in the midst of much development. Extensive salt marshes, with their salt hay, cord-grass, and pine-oak forests are interspersed with Atlantic white cedar swamps, maple-gum swamps, and successional fields. Close to 300 plant species grow in the park, which also supports an amazing assortment of creatures.

Viewing Information: Start at Cooper Environmental Center by picking up a park map and tree identification guide. The center has an observation deck with a boardwalk which overlooks a salt marsh. Actually, wildlife viewing can begin within 2 feet of the parking lot and continue throughout a hike over the 6 miles of trails. Over 250 species of birds live on Cattus Island. Ospreys nest in the summer, waterfowl migrate through in the fall and spring, and songbirds, raptors, and wading birds spend the year here. Look for buffleheads, canvasbacks, brants, mergansers, warblers, sharp-shinned hawks, and great blue herons on your walks. River otters are spotted early in the morning, along with white-tailed deer. Signs of nocturnal creatures such as raccoons, striped skunks, and Virginia opossums are visible in the daylight. Little brown bats and reptiles hibernate through winter but are commonly seen in the summer.

Directions: *From New Jersey 37 in Dover Township, take County Road Spur 549 (Fischer Boulevard) north for 2 miles to Cattus Island Boulevard. Turn right and follow signs to Cooper Environmental Center for 1 mile.*

Ownership: Ocean County Parks and Recreation (732) 270-6960

Size: 530 acres   **Closest Town:** Silverton

COASTAL REGION

The common snipe is the only snipe to nest in New Jersey. Similar to the American woodcock, it prefers wetter areas such as wet meadows, the boggy edges of marshes, or stream edges. LEONARD LEE RUE III

93

48. ISLAND BEACH STATE PARK AND BARNEGAT LIGHTHOUSE STATE PARK

Description: Island Beach is one of the few undeveloped barrier beaches on the Atlantic Coast and provides quite a contrast to the resort towns passed through on the way to the entrance. Sand dunes extend from the entrance of the park to the tip of the island at Barnegat Inlet. Barnegat Lighthouse, on Long Beach Island, is across the inlet from the southernmost point of Island Beach. Try the canoe trips in the summer, or take in the interpretive programs on the natural history of the island that are given daily throughout the summer and on weekends during spring and fall. Aeolium Nature Center at the Northern Natural Area is open year-round.

Viewing Information: The Southern Natural Area has a bird blind on Barnegat Bay, which makes winter waterfowl watching more comfortable. Park at Lot #20 for the trail to the bird blind or the canoe and kayak launch. On the Barnegat Bay side of the island, summer canoe tours through the tidal marsh and Sedge Island area allow you to see a variety of wildlife including ospreys, peregrine falcons, and wading birds. Birding is best in spring and summer, when the nesting black skimmers and common and least terns arrive. The jetty at Barnegat Lighthouse is a must-walk for the serious birder, no matter how cold it is in winter. Look for harlequin ducks, old squaws, and purple sandpipers. Bottlenosed dolphins and whales are sometimes visible from the beach, May–September, and harbor and gray seals, especially visible from the jetty areas, are regular visitors to New Jersey's waters in the winter. Year-round sightings of red foxes are common.

Directions: *From Toms River, take New Jersey 37 east to Seaside Heights. Turn right (south) on Central Avenue to Seaside Park and the entrance to Island Beach State Park. From the intersection of the Garden State Parkway and NJ 37, it is 10 miles to the entrance of the park. The park extends for 9.5 miles. To get to Barnegat Lighthouse, return on NJ 37 to U.S. Highway 9 in Toms River and travel south to Manahawkin. Take NJ 72 east to Long Beach Island. Turn left (north) and take Long Beach Boulevard, which becomes Central Avenue in the town of Barnegat Light. Drive north to Broadway. Follow Broadway left at the Y intersection and continue to the end of the island.*

Ownership: NJDEP Division of Parks and Forestry (732) 793-0506

Size: 3,000 acres **Closest Town:** Seaside Park

Ghost crabs remain beneath the sand during the heat of the day. They venture out from dusk to dawn and scurry around the beach looking for a meal.
CLAY MYERS

94

49. GREAT BAY BOULEVARD WILDLIFE MANAGEMENT AREA

Description: A 4-mile-long peninsula separates Great Bay and Little Egg Harbor at the mouth of the Mullica River where it meets the Little Egg Inlet to the Atlantic Ocean. It is an excellent area for birding in all seasons. The boulevard travels straight across this spit of land, offering vistas over the salt marsh to your left and right. Narrow, sandy beaches at the end of the peninsula provide additional birding opportunities.

Viewing Information: From the parking area at the end of the peninsula, walk to the edge of the bay with your binoculars and spotting scopes for views of the wintering rafts of waterfowl on the bay. Look for mergansers, buffleheads, and old squaws. Crabs, mussels, and clams are right at your feet, especially at low tide. Stop anywhere along the road to scan the marshes and mud flats for sandpipers, willets, plovers, yellowlegs, oystercatchers, black skimmers, and ospreys in the spring, summer, and fall. Look for brant in the fall and winter, and American black ducks, northern harriers, gulls, and terns anytime. Do not stop on the one-way bridges along the boulevard; there are plenty of places to pull off. Natural area with no facilities. OPEN FOR HUNTING DURING PRESCRIBED SEASONS.

Directions: *From U.S. Highway 9 in Tuckerton, turn southeast on Great Bay Boulevard. South Green Street Park, administered by Ocean County, is located within 3 miles, at the first bridge. Travel another 0.3 mile to the boundary of the wildlife management area. The parking lot is 3.7 miles from the WMA sign at the end of the road.*

Ownership: NJDEP, Division of Fish, Game, and Wildlife (609) 259-2132

Size: 5,346 acres   **Closest Town:** Tuckerton

Once endangered by the pesticide DDT, ospreys are on the rebound on New Jersey's coast. Intensive management by Division biologists and volunteers include the placement and maintenance of nesting platforms like those scattered throughout Great Bay. The platforms substitute for nest trees lost to coastal development.

RAY DAVIS

50. EDWIN B. FORSYTHE NATIONAL WILDLIFE REFUGE

Description: From the Brigantine Division of the Refuge, the Atlantic City skyline looms to the south across salt meadows and Reeds Bay. A preserved piece of the diminishing southern New Jersey coastal habitat, bay and tidal marshes comprise the majority of the refuge. The headquarters and public use facilities are on the edge of the refuge, which offers one of the best places in the country to see the ever-popular snow goose migration. Huge numbers of waterfowl make a stop here.

Viewing Information: The best bird-watching opportunities are during spring and fall migrations. The main attraction here is the 8-mile Wildlife Drive, a driving loop around impoundments with two observation towers. Thousands of wading birds and shorebirds use the impoundments, tidal creeks, and mud flats for feeding and resting during spring and fall migrations. Take particular note of the peregrine falcons, often seen sitting on the tower between the west and east pools. Most people view the birds from their cars, which act effectively as bird blinds. However, there are two foot trails. Leeds Trail, a 0.5-mile loop through salt marsh and native woods, is, in part, boardwalked and barrier-free. Akers Woodland Trail is a 0.25-mile loop through upland forest. Wildlife Drive brochures and bird checklists are available at the self-service information booth. Avoid the summer biting-fly season.

Directions: *From U.S. Highway 9 in Oceanville, turn east onto Great Creek Road and follow the signs to the refuge entrance in 0.6 mile.*

Ownership: U.S. Fish and Wildlife Service (609) 652-1665

Size: 42,000 acres   **Closest Town:** Oceanville

Forsythe's coastal wetlands provide a primary stopover and wintering location for hundreds of thousands of migratory waterfowl each year. LEN RUE, JR.

PINELANDS

Historically known as the Pine Barrens, early European settlers called this area barren because they could not grow their familiar crops in the acidic soils. The Pinelands region contains the most extensive wilderness tract on the mid-Atlantic seaboard: rising fewer than 100 feet above sea level, the Pinelands lie in a broad, flat surface within New Jersey's outer coastal plain. Bordered on the east by the Atlantic coast and on the west by a cuesta, or low ridge, the Pinelands encompass almost 1.4 million acres. An aquifer said to contain 17

trillion gallons of water lies beneath the sands. Over the course of geologic history, this portion of the state was alternately submerged and exposed as large oceans were frozen into glaciers during the ice ages and released again during warming periods. It is believed that because of this constant disruption, the plants and animals of the Pinelands developed here within the last 12,000 years (since the last ice age).

Human influence has had a deleterious effect on the Pinelands; there is probably not a single undisturbed acre remaining. In the past, the Pinelands produced a variety of industrial and agricultural products: iron ore, glass, lumber, sand, gravel, paper, turpentine, and sphagnum moss were exported from the late 1600s through the early 1900s. Blueberries and cranberries are the main exports today.

As the sizable timber supply was depleted by lumbering, residents turned to making charcoal. Charcoal was the fuel for firing the bog iron and glass furnaces. The woods were clearcut to obtain enough timber to operate the large charcoal pits, and vast acreages of woodlands were cleared as a result. As wood became scarce, people abandoned many of the Pinelands towns that had relied on the lumber industry or needed charcoal to fuel their furnaces. When people disappeared from the Pines, the forests gradually returned.

Today, the Pinelands are relatively undisturbed, though many of the plants and animals remain endangered. The area is protected as the Pinelands National Reserve, overseen by the Pinelands Commission, which limits development and provides safeguards for endangered and threatened species, adding a measure of protection against contamination and overuse of the aquifer.

The Pinelands' many tea-colored streams and rivers provide ample opportunities to explore by canoe, perhaps the best way to experience the flavor and unique ecosystems of this wild area. Visitors can also enjoy hiking and camping in addition to watching wildlife.

Left: In New Jersey, the endangered Pine Barrens tree frog is restricted to the Pinelands region. The next closest state where this frog is found is North Carolina. Listen for its "quonk-quonk-quonk" call in late spring in and around the acid waters of peat bogs and swamps where it breeds and lays its eggs. JEFF LEPORE

Preceding page: Cedar swamps are highly acidic and low in nutrients, creating a harsh environment for plants and animals. Most flora and fauna of the cedar swamp are specially adapted to live under these stressful conditions. Many species, like sundews, pitcher plants, and curly grass fern, flourish here.
DWIGHT HISCANO

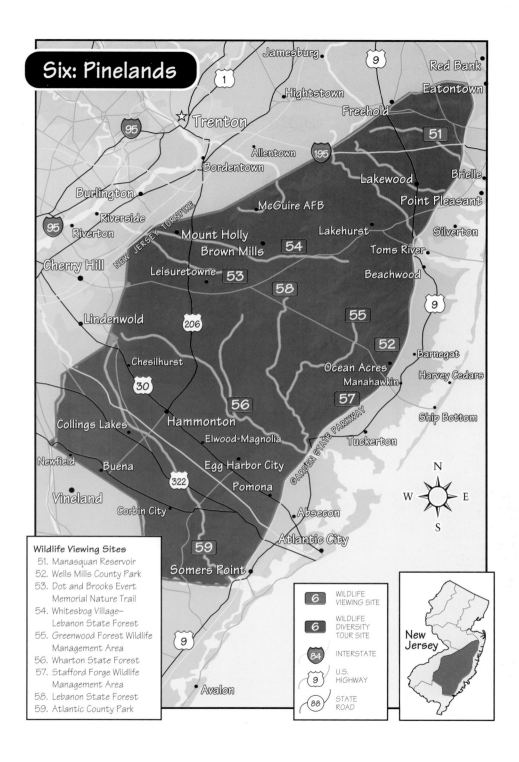

Six: Pinelands

Jamesburg

Red Bank

Eatontown

Hightstown

Freehold

Trenton

Allentown

Lakewood

Brielle

Bordentown

McGuire AFB

Point Pleasant

Burlington

Riverside

Lakehurst

Silverton

Riverton

Mount Holly

Lakehurst

Toms River

Brown Mills

54

Cherry Hill

Leisuretowne

53

Beachwood

58

Lindenwold

55

52

Barnegat

Chesilhurst

Ocean Acres

Harvey Cedars

Manahawkin

30

57

Ship Bottom

56

Hammonton

Elwood-Magnolia

Tuckerton

Collings Lakes

Newfield

Buena

Egg Harbor City

322

Pomona

Vineland

Corbin City

Absecon

Atlantic City

59

Somers Point

NEW JERSEY TURNPIKE

GARDEN STATE PARKWAY

N
W · E
S

Wildlife Viewing Sites

51. Manasquan Reservoir
52. Wells Mills County Park
53. Dot and Brooks Evert Memorial Nature Trail
54. Whitesbog Village–Lebanon State Forest
55. Greenwood Forest Wildlife Management Area
56. Wharton State Forest
57. Stafford Forge Wildlife Management Area
58. Lebanon State Forest
59. Atlantic County Park

6 WILDLIFE VIEWING SITE

6 WILDLIFE DIVERSITY TOUR SITE

84 INTERSTATE

9 U.S. HIGHWAY

88 STATE ROAD

New Jersey

Avalon

SUNDEW

CRANBERRY

HIGHBUSH BLUEBERRY

SWAMP MAPLE

FLYING SQUIRREL

PINE WARBLER

GRAY FOX

SAW-WHET OWL

EASTERN BLUEBIRD

PINE BARRENS TREE FROG

PITCHER PLANT

The Pinelands are characterized by pitch pine lowland forests, pine-oak upland forests, pygmy pine forests, Atlantic white cedar swamps, and hardwood swamps. While plant and animal life is not considered diverse, there are significant species unique to the Pinelands ecosystem. The Pine Barrens gentian, sundew, pitcher plant, Pine Barrens tree frog, and northern pine snake are a few examples. Many southern species of plants and animals reach their northern limit in the Pinelands.

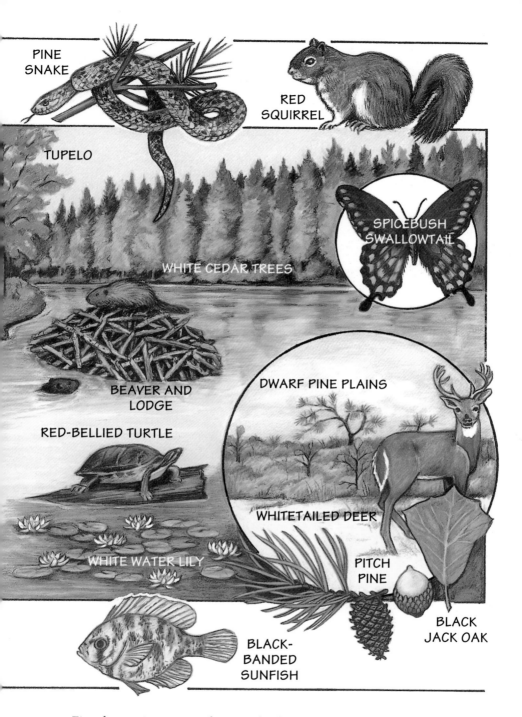

PINE SNAKE

RED SQUIRREL

TUPELO

SPICEBUSH SWALLOWTAIL

WHITE CEDAR TREES

BEAVER AND LODGE

RED-BELLIED TURTLE

DWARF PINE PLAINS

WHITETAILED DEER

WHITE WATER LILY

PITCH PINE

BLACK JACK OAK

BLACK-BANDED SUNFISH

Fire plays an important role in Pinelands ecology by burning off the forest litter and leaving the earth exposed. Pine seeds need heat to be released from their cones and bare earth in which to take root and grow. One theory is that the pygmy pine's dominance over the oak is a direct result of the area's frequent burns. Most Pinelands plants are fire resistant and can resprout from roots or larger limbs. Their emerging shoots provide food for wildlife.

51. MANASQUAN RESERVOIR

Description: The Manasquan Reservoir is in a mixed residential and agricultural region. A large, open body of water, the reservoir is unusual in the Pinelands, just as the Manasquan River is not a typical Pinelands stream. This may be explained by the fact that the reservoir is at the extreme northern end of the Pinelands, almost outside of the region.

Viewing Information: There is a well-marked access for the 5-mile perimeter trail that skirts the reservoir. There are good views of resident ducks year-round, migratory waterfowl in the fall, and an occasional bald eagle in winter. Take the trail in any season to see upland wildlife, wetlands species, and waterfowl on the reservoir. The second-floor observation deck on the visitor center is a good spot for wildlife watching.

Directions: *From Interstate 195, take exit 28 to New Jersey 9 north. Travel on NJ 9 north to Georgia Tavern Road. Turn right and proceed to Windler Road. Turn right and proceed to the reservoir entrance on your left.*

Ownership: Monmouth County Park System (732) 938-6760, 919-0996

Size: 1,203 acres (plus the 720-acre reservoir)

Closest Town: Farmingdale

The box turtle is primarily a forest species but is often seen near clearings, especially after summer rain showers. Here it forages on fruits like strawberry, raspberry, and blueberry. LEONARD LEE RUE III

Description: Extensive pine-oak forests are interrupted by Atlantic white cedar swamps and hardwood swamps of red (swamp) maple and sour gum trees. Wells Mills Lake, like all lakes in the Pinelands, is manmade.

Viewing Information: The park has 10 miles of hiking trails and an observation deck in the nature center that offers a view of the lake. White-tailed deer, raccoons, red and gray foxes, Fowler's toads, northern fence lizards, eastern hognose snakes, and eastern box turtles are all residents here. Tundra swans frequent the lake in the fall, along with ducks during migration. The park is open from 8 A.M. to sunset every day, while the nature center is open from 10 A.M. to 4 P.M. Rent a canoe, or take the 0.7 mile walk from the nature center to a waterfowl observation blind. There is also a short trail for the visually impaired, which uses a guide rope and tape player to indicate special objects to be felt, smelled, or heard.

Directions: *From the junction of New Jersey 72 and County Route 532, travel 3.5 miles on CR 532 to park entrance on right.*

Ownership: Ocean County (609) 971-3085

Size: 900 acres   **Closest Town:** Waretown

Fence lizards occupy a wide variety of habitats in the Pinelands. Most active in the mornings and evenings, these handsome creatures dart quickly toward cover when surprised. In late summer, young lizards emerge from eggs laid in the soil.
ROBERT T. ZAPPALORTI

PINELANDS

53. DOT AND BROOKS EVERT MEMORIAL NATURE TRAIL

Description: The Dot and Brooks Evert Memorial Nature Trail provides a rare opportunity to walk into the heart of an old swamp forest. In addition, this site vividly depicts the transition from inner coastal plain to Pinelands ecosystems. The mature hardwood forest showcases diverse populations of interior forest species, including several varieties of ferns and orchids. A mixed-hardwood oak forest characterizes the vegetation of the inner coastal plain while Atlantic white cedar, red maple, sour gum, and pitch pine are characteristic of the Pinelands.

Diversity Tour Information: This viewing site contains an "ecotone," an area where two distinctly different biotic communities, in this case inner coastal plain and Pinelands, blend. In this ecotone, there are plant and animal species from both regions, resulting in a highly diverse floodplain forest.

Explore the habitats by picking up a trail guide at the entrance and walking the Nature Trail. At Stop-the-Jade Run, Station 3 on the nature trail, you stand near the boundary of two different ecological regions. Upstream, the Pinelands' sand spreads across the outer coastal plain. Downstream, the rich, older soils of the inner coastal plain provide nutrients for the forests and farms of the Delaware Valley. Because of the richer soils, the mature hardwood forest of the inner coastal plain features swamp white oak, beech, sweet birch, and sweet gum trees. The sandy soils of Pinelands lowland communities are home to Atlantic white cedar, pitch pine, holly, and sweetbay magnolia trees. Where these two forest types are mixed together, look for prothonotary warblers that find cover in the dense thickets along the stream and hooded warblers, which prefer mature deciduous stands of red maple and sour gum.

Take the boardwalk loop trail along the floodplain and through forested wetlands for excellent songbird viewing in the spring. The forested stream corridor here is long and wide enough to support populations of some migratory forest songbirds. In addition to prothonotary and hooded warblers, look in the swamp forest for Kentucky warblers, white-eyed vireos, blue-winged and worm-eating warblers, and ovenbirds. Rough green snakes are abundant here, but difficult to detect. Look for signs of flying squirrels and long-tailed weasels.

The health of this forested floodplain depends on a number of things, many of which lie beyond this ecosystem. Conservation of nearby open space is important and water quality protection upstream is necessary for the continued health of this ecosystem. Runoff from development brings toxins and sediments which can alter the growth of vegetation and change wildlife habitat.

Towering above you in the old swamp forest are red maples, sour gum, willow oaks, and sassafras. Seeds from these trees are an important food for the area's wildlife. Sassafras berries shine purple on red stems in the fall, attracting migrating warblers like Swainson's thrush. Migratory songbirds are attracted to sour gum trees, which are also called black gum or tupelo. Hermit thrushes, scarlet tanagers, and red-eyed vireos, in addition to gray foxes and opossums, eat the fruit in the fall. Squirrels and chipmunks store maple seeds in their food caches, while prairie warblers favor young oaks as nesting sites. Six species of oak inhabit the forest: southern red, blackjack, willow, white, northern red, and swamp white. The acorns of white oaks are the best source of food for woodpeckers, eastern towhees, flying squirrels, and gray and red foxes. Wood ducks and mallards eat the seeds of willow oaks, which grow near water.

Pinelands shrubs such as blueberry and leatherleaf grow in the wettest areas, along with sweet pepperbush and small trees like persimmons, magnolias, and American hollys. American robins and cedar waxwings feed on the sugar-rich berries of the holly during the winter months. Worm-eating warblers are tiny forest birds that prefer the dense understory shrubs, which grow in slightly drier soils.

Directions: *From the junction of New Jersey routes 70 and 72 (traffic circle), take the Pemberton, Fort Dix, Mount Holly exit and travel 2.3 miles on Ongs Hat Road to a left turn on the first sharp curve immediately before a small tavern. Travel 1.4 miles to a small parking area on your right.*

Wildlife Diversity Tour Directions:

FROM DOT AND BROOKS EVERT MEMORIAL TRAIL (SITE 53)
TO WHITESBOG VILLAGE (SITE 54)

From Dot and Brooks Evert Memorial Nature Trail, turn left out of the parking lot and travel 3.7 miles on Ongs Hat Road to 4 mile circle (intersection of New Jersey routes 70 and 72). Take NJ 70 east for approximately 8 miles to County Route 530. Turn left and take CR 530 west for 1.2 miles. Turn right into the entrance to Whitesbog Village and continue 0.5 mile to parking area.

Ownership: New Jersey Conservation Foundation (908) 234-1225

Size: 170 acres   **Closest Town:** Pemberton Borough

Cedar waxwings are fruit-eating birds. Flocks of waxwings often descend on an area to feed on ripe berries only to disappear just as suddenly when the fruit is gone. Waxwings nest late in the season to ensure a plentiful food source for their young. JEFF LEPORE

Description: Whitesbog Village, a historic cranberry and blueberry farming village, has been restored to depict life in the Pines in the early 1900s. Inactive cranberry bogs and blueberry fields are in different stages of succession, while active bogs provide an example of cranberry farming. Winter flooding of bogs attracts a large population of tundra swans. Lebanon State Forest's vegetation is mainly upland pine-oak forest.

Diversity Tour Information: The 31,879-acre Lebanon State Forest is located in the heart of New Jersey's Pinelands. It is named after the Lebanon Glass Works, which was a thriving Pinelands industry between 1851 and 1867. Abundant sand and locally produced charcoal made the manufacture of high quality window glass possible. However, once the timber supply for charcoal-making was exhausted, the factory was abandoned and the site of the glass-works was reclaimed by the forest. Over a century ago, cranberry cultivation was introduced to the area.

Whitesbog Village is a turn-of-the-century agricultural settlement, built by the Joseph J. White Company as the center of its cranberry and blueberry farming operation. Purchased by the state in the late 1960s, the Joseph J. White company still cultivates many of the old cranberry bogs and blueberry fields. Many of the homes are leased as private residences or by environmental and educational organizations.

The Whitesbog Preservation Trust, a nonprofit group, seeks to preserve the village of Whitesbog and surrounding ecosystems through education, interpretation, and recreation. Be sure to pick up a self-guided nature trail description and a schedule of guided nature tours and special programs at the trust office. An annual Blueberry Festival is held in Whitesbog Village each June.

The cranberry is one of only two native American fruits grown in wetlands. The other is the blueberry. The Lenape Indians were the first people to harvest cranberries in New Jersey. They used the wild red berry for food, medicine, and as a symbol of peace. Cranberry growth and survival depends on a fragile combination of wetlands soils, geology, and climate. They are a perennial crop and it is not unusual to find 75 to 100-year-old bogs still in cultivation.

Cranberry wetlands recharge and filter groundwater, control floods, and retain storm water. Abandoned bogs provide diverse habitat for a variety of birds and animals, including bald eagles, great blue herons, ospreys, and wild turkeys, and plants, including Pine Barrens bellwort and pitcher plants.

Examples of upland and wetland vegetation abound within the forest. Dense stands of Atlantic white cedar, one of the region's most characteristic trees, are found along the forest's streams. The pine-oak woods are a favorite nesting place for redheaded woodpeckers and home to pine, corn, and scarlet snakes. The acidic bogs host a variety of unique plants including orchids, sun-dews, and pitcher plants.

Pine warblers arrive in March, followed by eastern bluebirds, eastern (rufous-sided) towhees, tree swallows, and whip-poor-wills, all of which are common nesters. With some patience, you might see little and big brown bats, white-tailed deer, red and gray foxes, and red squirrels. Nowhere else in New

Jersey can you observe tundra swans at such close range. View these magnificent swans from your car by following any of the old bog roads leading out of the village. The swans at Whitesbog prefer the abandoned, flooded cranberry bogs. In February, over 500 swans can be seen.

BE CAREFUL DRIVING ON SANDY ROADS. NO TRESPASSING ON ACTIVE CRANBERRY BOGS.

Directions: *Whitesbog Village: from the junction of New Jersey 70 and County Route 530, take CR 530 west towards Browns Mills for 1.2 miles. Turn right at the entrance to Whitesbog Village and continue 0.5 mile to parking area. Lebanon State Forest Visitor Center: take Route 72 east at the Four Mile Circle. Turn left at mile marker 1. Take the first right and the center will be on your left.*

Wildlife Diversity Tour Directions:
FROM WHITESBOG VILLAGE (SITE 54) TO GREENWOOD FOREST WMA (SITE 55)

From Whitesbog Village, take County Route 530 east to New Jersey 70. Turn right and proceed to 4 mile circle. At the circle, take New Jersey 72 and travel to County Route 539. Turn left onto CR 539 and proceed for 6.2 miles to Greenwood Forest WMA's Webbs Mill Bog on your right.

Ownership: NJDEP Division of Parks and Forestry. Lebanon State Forest (609) 726-1191; Whitesbog Preservation Trust (609) 893-4646

Size: Lebanon State Forest 31,879 acres, Whitesbog 3,000 acres

Closest Town: Browns Mills, Pemberton Township

A common sight in freshwater, eastern painted turtles can be seen basking in the sun on rocks, logs, and vegetation from spring through early fall. SIMON B. LEVENTHAL

Description: Most of this area is an upland pine-oak forest interspersed with a few hundred acres of fields. The lowlands contain pitch pine forests and Atlantic white cedar bogs. Three small lakes and wetlands provide habitat for waterfowl, fish, reptiles, and amphibians. An extensive system of sand roads provides ample opportunity for hiking and wildlife-watching.

Diversity Tour Information: Webb's Mill is a fine example of a Pinelands bog with its typical wetlands vegetation. Naturally absorbent sphagnum moss hummocks support a variety of Pinelands plants including sundews, St. Johnswort, cranberries, curly-grass ferns, orchids, dwarf huckleberries, and leatherleaf. Use the boardwalk and trail to observe plants and animals in the bog; otherwise you will quickly discover how easy it is to sink knee-deep in peat and water!

This is an ideal location for observing Pinelands reptiles and amphibians. Listen and look for Pine Barrens tree frogs in late spring and early summer, especially on warm, rainy nights. Endangered northern pine snakes and eastern timber rattlesnakes are residents of the wildlife management area. Songbirds typical of these pine-oak forests include pine warblers, Carolina chickadees, tufted titmice, and white-breasted nuthatches. Look for great blue herons in the wetlands during summer; and listen especially for eastern (rufous-sided) towhees, which are present throughout the area

The Pinelands support a community of plants and animals not found elsewhere in New Jersey. Many characteristic species are southern species that reach their northern limit here in New Jersey. The Pine Barrens tree frog, pine snake, and corn snake are three such species and are listed as endangered or threatened in New Jersey.

As a habitat for most animals, the Pine Barrens are indeed barren. The area's physical and biotic characteristics create a harsh environment with low habitat diversity, limiting the variety of animals found here. Fish and amphibians are especially limited because of the extreme acidity of the Pine Barrens' cedar water. However, there are certain amphibians that are well adapted to the area because of the tolerance they've developed to acidity. In fact, the Pinelands is the only place in New Jersey where carpenter frogs and Pine

Potential dinner fare for the three endangered Pinelands snakes (the corn snake, pine snake, and timber rattlesnake) the white-footed mouse thrives in wooded and brushy habitats. It is most vulnerable at the edges of clearings, which are attractive hunting and basking areas for the snakes.
BRECK P. KENT

Barrens tree frogs are found. All three major habitat types typical of the Pinelands occur in Greenwood Forest Wildlife Management Area: upland pine-oak forests, lowland cedar bogs, and acidic streams and ponds.

Reptiles are common throughout the Pinelands. The most common turtles are the terrestrial eastern box turtle and the aquatic painted, spotted, and snapping turtles. Stinkpot and red-bellied turtles are also frequently seen. The most common snakes are northern water snakes, scarlet snakes, black racers, eastern hognose snakes, common kingsnakes, milk snakes, and rough green snakes. The area's sandy soil attracts burrowing snakes such as pine, scarlet, hognose, and worm snakes.

Pinelands mammals include white-tailed deer, eastern cottontails, eastern moles, masked shrews, and red squirrels. Southern flying squirrels are numerous, but rarely seen. Several small rodents such as white-footed mice, woodland voles, red-backed voles, and meadow jumping mice are common.

Cedar swamps in the Greenwood Forest stabilize stream flow, temporarily storing floodwaters and mitigating the effects of droughts. They filter and purify water as it flows through them.

Cedar swamps are prime habitat for an endangered plant known as swamp pink. In addition, fringed orchids, turkey-beard, and curly grass ferns can be found around the edges of cedar swamps. Birds that nest in the area's cedar swamps include black-throated green warblers, black-and-white warblers, brown creepers, ovenbirds, and hermit thrushes. Southern red-backed voles are the predominant small mammals; fungal spores in their fecal pellets suggest that they play a role in dispersing mycorrhizal fungi, which is important for the successful growth of cedars. Water-filled hollows under the roots of cedars are used as winter dens by eastern timber rattlesnakes.

The Greenwood Forest Wildlife Management Area is a natural area with no facilities. BE CAREFUL DRIVING ON SANDY ROADS. OPEN FOR HUNTING DURING PRESCRIBED SEASONS.

Directions: *From the junction of New Jersey 72 and County Route 539, turn north on CR 539. Proceed approximately 6.2 miles to the pulloff for Webb's Mill Bog on your right. The trail begins immediately on your right. To get to the small lakes and wetlands, look for the Greenwood WMA sign 0.9 mile east of CR 539 on NJ 72. Turn left into the WMA at the sign. Within a mile, turn right onto any of the sand trails and park. Walk east to the lakes.*

Wildlife Diversity Tour Directions:

FROM GREENWOOD FOREST WMA (SITE 55) TO WHARTON STATE FOREST (SITE 56)

From Greenwood Forest WMA, take County Route 539 to New Jersey 72. Turn right and proceed to County Route 532. Turn left onto CR 532 and follow it approximately 4.5 miles to County Route 563. Turn left (south) on CR 563 and travel several miles to County Route 542. Turn right on CR 542 and travel 6 miles to the entrance to Batsto Visitor Center on the right.

Ownership: NJDEP Division of Fish, Game, and Wildlife (609) 259-2132

Size: 24,726 acres   **Closest Town:** Whiting

56. WHARTON STATE FOREST

Description: Wharton State Forest, encompassing nearly 110,000 acres in the heart of the Pinelands, is the largest tract of public land in New Jersey. The Atsion Recreation Area, Batsto Village, four rivers, and hundreds of miles of sandy hiking trails and roads are some of the attractions within the forest. Batsto Village is a reconstruction of a Pinelands village that was active for several centuries.

Diversity Tour Information: The Pinelands are a truly special place. Unbroken forests of pine, oak, and cedar make the Pinelands the largest tract of open space on the mid-Atlantic coast. In 1978, 934,000 acres in the Pinelands were designated as the Pinelands National Reserve to protect their unique natural and cultural resources.

The Pinelands' uniqueness springs from its water. The sandy soil allows water to pass through quickly and be stored in the aquifer below. Slow moving streams, fed by the 17-trillion-gallon Cohansey Aquifer, supply the marshes and bays of southern New Jersey with water. Although the aquifer may be as deep as 70 feet, it frequently reaches ground level and percolates up as a swamp, river, or bog. Rain that falls in the Pines takes on acid from the pine needles on the trees and the detritus on the forest floor, before leaching the iron from the sand to eventually form bog iron.

One of the best ways to experience the Pinelands is by canoe. Miles of river run through Wharton State Forest and more than a dozen nearby outfitters offer canoe rentals. Among the waterways you can travel are the Batsto, Mullica, Oswego, Great Egg Harbor, and Wading rivers, as well as Cedar Creek. The rides are calm, although the switchback curves may provide some challenge to the novice paddler.

Only a select variety of plants and animals are able to tolerate the acidic streams of Wharton State Forest. Look in the vegetation at the margins of lakes and in the backwaters of streams for the brightly colored blackbanded sunfish. Another interesting Pinelands fish is the eastern mudminnow, which hides in dense vegetation. The mudminnow is a facultative air-breather, which means that although it has gills for breathing under water, it can also survive during periods of low water by using its gas bladder to breathe air. The aquatic larvae of northern red salamanders are plentiful in Pinelands streams; look for adults that remain near the streams' margins to guard the developing young. Be aware of gnawed trees along the rivers, evidence of beaver activity. River otters and long-tailed weasels are rarely seen, but are present along the streams. Raccoons and gray foxes are also common throughout the area .

Batsto Village is a restored town that was first settled in 1766, around a bog iron furnace. The village consists of 33 historic buildings and structures, and an interpretive center, which offers exhibits and programs about the natural resources of the Pinelands. Call for information. There is also a self-guided, 1.5-mile nature walk around the lake, through a variety of pine forests, pine-oak woods, Atlantic white cedar bogs, and red maple swamp habitats.

Listen for the cheery *"drink your tea"* of the eastern (rufous-sided) towhee as it searches noisily for food amongst fallen leaves. Other common birds of the upland areas include blue jays, Carolina chickadees, pine warblers, prairie warblers, black-and-white warblers, ovenbirds, brown thrashers, ruffed grouse, and bobwhite quail. Look in low areas of dense vegetation along streams or rivers for catbirds, yellow warblers, yellowthroats, American red-starts, and field sparrows. Herons, egrets, and ducks frequent the rivers and lakes. Redwing blackbirds, swamp sparrows, and song sparrows live among the emergent vegetation surrounding lakes.

Although not a formal tourist center, visitors are permitted to walk the site of old Atsion Village. The Greek Revival mansion built in 1826 stands like a roadside sentinel at the site of the once thriving village. The Atsion Recreation Center, on the opposite side of Route 206, consists of a public beach, rental cabins, a nature trail, and picnic area, and is open April 1 through October 31.

Pink blazes clearly mark the 50-mile-long Batona Trail, which stretches from Ong's Hat in Lebanon State Forest, through Batsto and the Wharton State Forest, to Coal Road in Bass River State Forest. The trail crosses several roads and can be reached by car at many points, making it possible to enjoy different types and lengths of hikes. On your hike, look for orchids, huckleberries,

Opposite: *The white-tailed deer is New Jersey's most abundant large mammal. Does give birth to one or two fawns in June.* LEONARD LEE RUE III

white-tailed deer, and numerous raptors. Trail maps, restrooms, drinking water, and parking facilities are available at park headquarters.

OPEN FOR HUNTING IN PRESCRIBED AREAS.

Directions: *For information and maps, drive to Batsto Visitor Center first. From U.S. Highway 30 in Hammonton, take County Route 542 east for 8 miles. The entrance to the village is on the left. To reach Atsion Village and Recreation Area: From the intersection of US 206 and US 30 in Hammonton, travel 7.5 miles north on US 206. The entrance is on the left.*

Wildlife Diversity Tour Directions:

FROM WHARTON STATE FOREST (SITE 56) TO STAFFORD FORGE WMA (SITE 57)

From the Batsto Visitor Center in Wharton State Forest, take County Route 542 east to the Garden State Parkway. Take the Garden State Parkway north to exit 58. Take County Route 539 north for 0.2 mile. Turn right at mile marker 4 and travel 1.6 miles to the Stafford Forge WMA entrance straight ahead.

Ownership: NJDEP Division of Parks and Forestry. Wharton State Forest Headquarters (609) 561-3262; Atsion Ranger Station (609) 268-0444.

Size: 108,773 acres   **Closest Town:** Hammonton

This brightly colored and attractive northern red salamander spends its entire life in or near water. The aquatic larvae develop in water and venture onto land. Adults rarely leave the water's edge. BRECK P. KENT

Description: Four ponds, a small freshwater marsh, and hundreds of acres of pine-oak forest provide a haven from the developed areas nearby for nesting, migrating, and wintering wildlife. A unique pygmy pine forest covers the northern end of the wildlife management area.

Diversity Tour Information: Pine-oak forests predominate the Stafford Forge Wildlife Management Area, offering important habitat for nesting, migrating, and wintering wildlife. Pitch pine, blackjack oak, and southern white cedar are the primary trees in this ecosystem. Pitch pine can grow in distinctly different settings, from the very driest to the wettest. Most of the other trees, shrubs, herbs, mosses, and lichens, however, live in either the uplands or the wetlands where soils are saturated part of the year. The abundant moisture in the wetland sites supports dense vegetation and reduces its flammability.

The existence of the unique plant and animal communities at Stafford Forge Wildlife Management Area is linked to the fact that, historically, fires have not been rare here. Native Americans burned the woods extensively to improve hunting conditions and, until the early 1900s, the forest was clearcut by farmers and other residents, every 25 to 50 years, for firewood, charcoal, poles, and lumber. Over time, the cycle of burning and cutting eliminated many plants that had grown along the margins. The absence of these potential competitors and the stimulation caused by the fires favored the plants we see in the Pinelands today, many of which are rare elsewhere. As is typical of unusual forest types, a unique assortment of plants and animals, including the curly grass fern, broom crowberry, eastern timber rattlesnake, and the Pine Barrens tree frog live in this managed area.

For species to thrive in a fire-prone area, individuals of that species must either survive fires, or produce young that become established after the fire. Blueberries, pitch pines, and oaks have underground stems or roots that are able to survive fires. The above-ground parts of the plant may be killed, but after the fire they are regenerated. The pitch pine, which is prevalent in the Pinelands, has developed special adaptations to deal with frequent fires. In addition to sprouting from their roots, they have serotinous cones, which only open to disperse their seeds after a fire, ensuring that their lightweight seeds will come in contact with the bare earth they need in order to sprout. The trunks of pitch pines may be scorched during a fire, but the thick bark prevents the fire from killing the underlying cambium layer. The trunk survives and produces buds under the bark, which grow into small branches. For animals to survive a fire, they typically must either burrow or flee.

The pygmy pine forest on the plains at the northern end of the wildlife management area is a dense stand of dwarf, but mature, pitch pine, blackjack oak, and scrub oak trees only 4 to 6 feet tall. The fire history of the area favors a race of pitch pine that is slow growing, but matures quickly and produces serotinous cones. Look for pyxie moss and false heather, which are abundant herbs throughout the pygmy forests. Most of the oak trees in the forest originated as sprouts after fires, and many have two or more trunks. The trunks of these trees are very susceptible to heart rot: the heart rot fungi and the excavations of carpenter ants weaken the trunks. The uppermost sections of many

PINELANDS

large oaks' crowns have been snapped off by strong winds and the lower branches have developed a new oddly shaped crown. These trees are important as nest and feeding sites for many wildlife species.

Travel north from the entrance to the wildlife management area by foot or car along the sand road. The road passes along the east side of a chain of four ponds. Each pond is separated by a dam, which you can walk or drive across. At the northern end of the last pond, near the marsh, there are trees that have been gnawed upon by beaver. Look for hognose snakes, southern leopard frogs, and northern water snakes in the spring and summer. Wintering birds include wood thrushes and American black ducks. Wood ducks and Canada geese frequent the ponds in all seasons. Near the margins of the ponds look for white water lilies, spatterdocks, bladderworts, and other submerged or floating leaf plants. Sphagnum mosses, sedges, rushes, pipeworts, chain ferns, and other emergent plants grow in water no deeper than a few inches. Lowland broomsedge, bullsedge, and other grasses grow in the small freshwater marsh.

The Stafford Ford Wildlife Management Area is a natural area with no facilities. BE CAREFUL DRIVING ON SAND ROADS. OPEN FOR HUNTING DURING PRESCRIBED SEASONS.

Directions: *From Garden State Parkway exit 58, take County Route 539 north for 0.2 mile. Turn right at the 4-mile marker. Go 1.6 miles to WMA entrance straight ahead. For the viewing platform in the pygmy pine forest, stay on CR 539 north toward Warren Grove for 2 more miles. The platform and trail are on the right.*

Ownership: NJDEP Division of Fish, Game, and Wildlife (609) 259-2132

Size: 17,010   **Closest Towns:** Stafford Forge, Eagleswood Township

Fire plays an important role in the life history of many Pinelands species. The pine snake needs forest openings as egg laying and foraging sites and does well in Pinelands areas where fires occur occasionally.
CLAY MYERS

58. LEBANON STATE FOREST

Description: Lebanon State Forest, located in the heart of the Pinelands, has 400 miles of roads for hiking and driving. Pakim Pond, once a cranberry bog, is now a 5-acre swimming hole. Whitesbog Village, described in site 55, is in Lebanon Forest. The Cedar Swamp Natural Area, surrounded by pitch pine forest, is an outstanding example of an Atlantic white cedar swamp. Rare orchids, sundews, and pitcher plants highlight the swamp. Check at the office for nature center hours. Cabins are available April 1 through October 31. The 50-mile-long Batona Hiking Trail starts in Ong's Hat in Lebanon Forest.

Viewing Information: Many of the birds, amphibians, and mammals common to the Pinelands can be seen in the Cedar Swamp Natural Area, located just to the south of the visitor center on the way to Pakim Pond. Several sand roads ring the area and the Batona Trail crosses part of it. Beaver are often busy in the area, white-tailed deer are common, and you may hear Pine Barrens treefrogs, carpenter frogs, and red squirrels. Birds of the pines and cedar swamps include pine warblers, prairie warblers, and white-eyed vireos. Scarlet tanagers and redheaded woodpeckers have been spotted nearby.

BE CAREFUL DRIVING ON SANDY ROADS. OPEN FOR HUNTING IN DESIGNATED AREAS DURING PRESCRIBED SEASONS.

Directions: *From the junction of New Jersey 70 and New Jersey 72, travel south 1.1 miles on NJ 72 to the state forest entrance on the left (east.) Stop at the office for trail maps, Batona Trail brochures, and information.*

Ownership: NJDEP Division of Parks and Forestry (609) 726-1191

Size: 32,012 acres   **Closest Town:** New Lisbon

The pine-oak forests of Lebanon State Forest provide plenty of acorns for the white-breasted nuthatch to feed on. This bird can be seen descending tree trunks head first, stopping often to glean insects from the bark.
DR. PETER J. LEKOS

59. ATLANTIC COUNTY PARK

Description: The Atlantic County Park in Estell Manor is at the site of a former WW I munitions factory and has now returned to its natural state. More than 18 miles of hiking trails follow abandoned railroad beds. Freshwater wetlands, ponds, creeks, upland fields, oak-pine and pine-oak forests, and hardwood swamps are accessible to those willing to hike. Special wildlife enhancement areas like the butterfly garden and Cribber's field attract Eastern bluebirds and the swallowtail, buckeye, and angelwing butterflies. Typical Pinelands reptiles and amphibians, including Pine Barrens tree frogs, northern pine snakes, and corn snakes live here, too.

Viewing Information: Duck Farm Road takes you to Tin Box Road and the dam of an energetic beaver, who may be working hard to cover the road with a pond. For a drier hike, take Frog Pond Road to a wildlife enhancement area and Swamp Trail. The 1.5-mile loop trail from the nature center winds through a hardwood swamp and upland forest and past several ponds. Turtles, frogs, snakes, and insects make their homes at the ponds from spring through early fall. Raccoons, white-tailed deer, and red foxes, whose dens are just off the trail, visit the ponds. The observation deck overlooking Stephens Creek is on the boundary between a freshwater marsh and the oak-pine forest. Ospreys and belted kingfishers are often seen fishing along the creek, and river otters use the bank as a slide. The swamps are alive in spring with neotropical songbirds. Ask at the Estell Manor Park office for directions to nearby sites, such as Lake Lenape in Mays Landing, where you can take an extended hike into a cedar swamp, and the wild and scenic Great Egg Harbor River, a great place to see eagles, ducks, and mergansers.

Directions: *From U.S. Highway 40 in Mays Landing, take New Jersey 50 south for 3.7 miles to the entrance of Estell Manor Park on the left. The nature center and parking area are on the right after a short distance.*

Ownership: Atlantic County, Division of Parks and Recreation (609) 645-5960

Size: 1,700 acres **Closest Town:** Mays Landing

Butterfly watching is becoming an increasingly popular pastime. Look for this tiger swallowtail near honeysuckle, phlox, thistle, and milkweed.
R. AL SIMPSON

LOWER DELAWARE RIVER

The Lower Delaware River Region lies within the inner coastal plain, separated from the outer coastal plain by a belt of low hills running southwest across the state from Sandy Hook to Lower Alloway. These hills are remnants of a landform called a cuesta, which rises to a height of nearly 400 feet in some areas. From this high point, the inner coastal plain slopes gradually south and west toward the Delaware River and Estuary. The Delaware, named in 1610 by Captain Samuel Argall for Virginia Governor Lord De La War, forms the western border of this region. Two ecologically distinct sections of the estuary are in the Lower Delaware Region: the freshwater tidal river from Trenton falls to Camden, and the brackish upper estuary from Camden to the Cohansey River. The estuary has numerous fresh and brackish water marshes and provides habitat for many species of birds, fishes, reptiles, amphibians, and mammals.

The soils of this region are made up of unconsolidated sands, silts, clays, and gravels. This soil is generally more fertile and moist, and less sandy, than that of the outer coastal plain. Soils in this area contain large amounts of glauconite or greensand marl. In some areas the mineral is so abundant that the soil is dark green. Much of this region serves as the transportation corridor between New York and Philadelphia, complete with the accompanying development. Land not developed is cleared and devoted to agriculture. Fruit, vegetable, dairy, and poultry farms dot the remaining open space, but these are disappearing at an alarming rate. As farms and fields are abandoned, they become small havens for eastern cottontails, ring-necked pheasants, woodchucks, garter snakes, and field sparrows.

As early as 1900, this area was reported to be only 15 percent wooded. For the most part, it is only the wetter lowlands that contain extensive tracts of natural vegetation. Virgin forest has disappeared and the woodlands that remain have been cut repeatedly since European settlement. The forests that are left are predominantly pine-oak on the drier, sandier soils, mixed-oak on the mesic uplands, and hardwood swamp forest in the low-lying wet areas. Many southern species of plants, like sweet gum, willow oak, Spanish oak, and persimmon, reach their northern limit on the inner coastal plain.

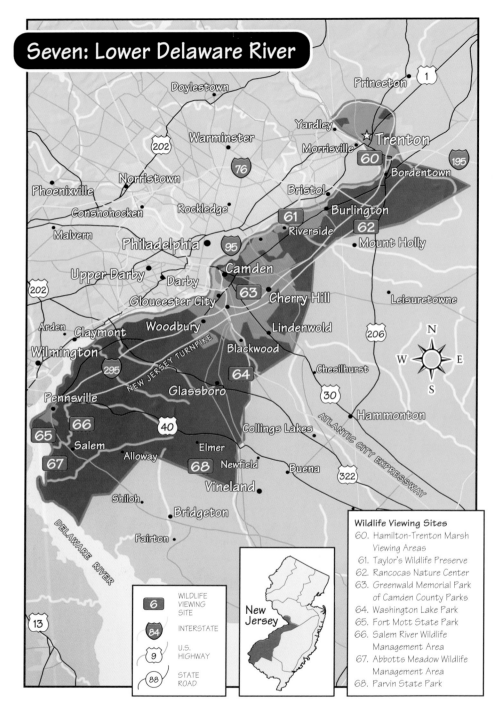

Seven: Lower Delaware River

Wildlife Viewing Sites
60. Hamilton-Trenton Marsh Viewing Areas
61. Taylor's Wildlife Preserve
62. Rancocas Nature Center
63. Greenwald Memorial Park of Camden County Parks
64. Washington Lake Park
65. Fort Mott State Park
66. Salem River Wildlife Management Area
67. Abbotts Meadow Wildlife Management Area
68. Parvin State Park

6 WILDLIFE VIEWING SITE
84 INTERSTATE
9 U.S. HIGHWAY
88 STATE ROAD

New Jersey

Preceding page: *Much of the wildlife activity of the salt marsh takes place along the tidal creeks. The tall salt marsh cordgrass provides ample shelter for wary salt marsh fauna.* CLAY MYERS

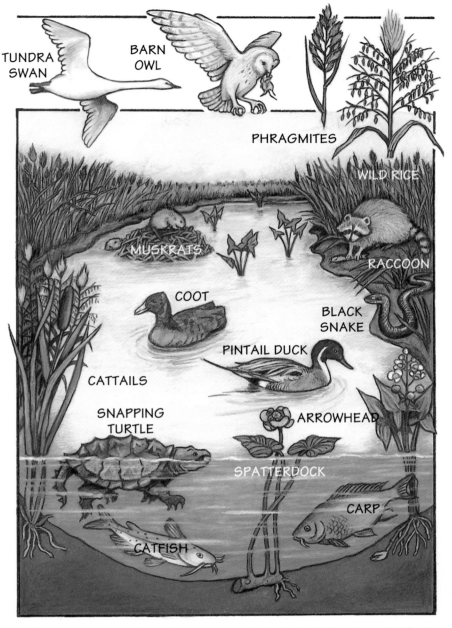

TUNDRA SWAN

BARN OWL

PHRAGMITES

WILD RICE

MUSKRATS

RACCOON

COOT

BLACK SNAKE

PINTAIL DUCK

CATTAILS

SNAPPING TURTLE

ARROWHEAD

SPATTERDOCK

CARP

CATFISH

The Lower Delaware River Region is dotted with both tidal and nontidal freshwater marshes. The marsh's productivity is legendary. An ample supply of sunlight, water, and nutrients from decaying plants and animals assure lush plant growth, which in turn provides food and shelter for many creatures throughout the year. Migratory waterfowl use marshes as stop-over areas. Raccoons fish for frogs, insects, and snails at the water's edge, while muskrats industriously repair their lodges. Hawks and owls can often be seen hunting the upland edge for rodents, reptiles, and amphibians. While the familiar cattail symbolizes the freshwater marsh, the phragmite, or common reed, is becoming more prevalent. Phragmites grow worldwide and are native to North America; however, they are invasive and tend to crowd out other, more beneficial marsh vegetation.

60. HAMILTON-TRENTON MARSH VIEWING AREAS

SPRING LAKE AND WATSON WOODS OF JOHN A. ROEBLING MEMORIAL PARK, PLUS THE SCENIC OVERLOOK ON THE DELAWARE RIVER

Description: Located in the densely developed region southeast of Trenton, in Hamilton Township, this is the northernmost freshwater tidal marsh on the Delaware River. Ponds, creeks, the Delaware and Raritan Canal, and the Delaware River are all connected by the marshland, which includes both tidal and nontidal marsh, forested swamp, and upland forest. These valuable wetlands are contiguous to the Crosswicks and Delaware River greenways.

Viewing Information: Two of the public accesses to the marsh are good places to view wildlife, canoe, and hike. Spring Lake was once part of the White City Amusement Park, and the remains of the ornate stone steps that linked a trolley stop at the top of the bluff to the park below are still visible today. The other public access, at the eastern end of John A. Roebling Memorial Park, includes the Watson House, the oldest standing home in Mercer County. A dirt trail connects one access area to the other.

Birding along the road is popular during spring migration. You may see yellow-throated vireos, black-and-white warblers, American redstarts, and scarlet tanagers in the wooded areas along the bluffs, and thrushes, tufted titmice, and chickadees in the thickets of mountain laurel.

At Spring Lake, walk west from the parking area along the causeway and around the wooded island or follow the path along the south edge of the lake.

Within the marsh, look for mergansers and double-crested cormorants in the winter, and ospreys, great blue herons, and wood ducks during the spring and summer. At the edges of the marsh areas, you are likely to see signs of muskrats, raccoons, and frogs. The Scenic Overlook from Interstate 295 gives you a view of the river and marsh. It is also a good spot to check out the wintering waterfowl and gulls on the Delaware River.

Directions: *John A. Roebling Memorial Park: From the traffic circle on U.S. Highway 206 (White Horse Circle), go toward Trenton on US 206 (Broad Street) for 1.5 miles to Sewell Avenue. Turn left (south) and continue on Sewell Avenue for 4 blocks to the old paved road entrance to Spring Lake, a left turn going downhill. The scenic overlook: From Sewell Avenue and US 206, go back east 0.3 mile to West Park Avenue. Turn right and follow it to Westcott Street, about 5 blocks. Turn left onto Wescott, then right at Watson House. Follow the road down the hill for parking and a picnic area. New Jersey Transit bus route 409 makes stops on US 206. The scenic overlook is on Interstate 295, 3.3 miles south of its junction with Interstate 195.*

Ownership: Mercer County Park Commission and NJ Department of Transportation; contact Delaware and Raritan Greenway (609) 924-4646 or their Marsh Hotline (609) 452-0525 for information.

Size: 1,250 acres   **Closest Towns:** Trenton, Hamilton, and Bordentown

61. TAYLOR'S WILDLIFE PRESERVE

Description: A privately-owned wildlife preserve, Taylor's is also the last farm along the Delaware River between Trenton and Camden. An organic, pick-your-own farm, rental gardens, freshwater wetlands, and ponds make up the protected refuge lands. Nearby industrial areas belie the presence of this gem. OPEN FROM SUNRISE TO SUNSET ONLY.

Viewing Information: Park at the trailhead for the Joseph H. Taylor Interpretive Trail at the end of the dirt road. The trail starts off with a magnificent view of the Delaware River. Take advantage of the benches and sit for a spell to watch ospreys and mallards, which frequent the river and the marsh at Wright Cove. Over 200 species of bird frequent the preserve, which is why the Delaware Valley Ornithological Club takes field trips here. Ask at the yellow house for a trail map. TAKE CARE NOT TO WALK OR DRIVE ON CROP FIELDS.

Directions: *From U.S. Highway 130 in Cinnaminson, take Taylor's Lane west. New Albany Road goes east from the same interchange. Travel on Taylor's Lane for 1.4 miles to River Road. Continue straight across River Road onto a dirt road. Drive about 1 mile past the homes, barns, and a vegetable stand to a parking area at the end of the road.*

Ownership: Sylvia Taylor; contact New Jersey Natural Lands Trust (609) 984-1339

Size: 89 acres   **Closest Town:** Cinnaminson

62. RANCOCAS NATURE CENTER

Description: North of the Rancocas Creek and adjacent to Rancocas State Park is a 130-year-old farmhouse. The farmhouse, turned into a nature center by the New Jersey Audubon Society, has a museum, bookshop, and classroom. The habitats protected here include a freshwater marsh, a mixed-oak forest, old fields, conifer plantations, and stands of American holly.

Viewing Information: Self-guided trails radiate out from the nature center into the adjoining parkland. Birding is best in May, but over 160 species of birds live in the area year-round. Red-tailed hawks and mammals such as white-tailed deer, red foxes, and muskrats are especially visible year-round. Wood ducks nest around the marshes from April to September, and Canada geese and other waterfowl are usually present in February and March.

Directions: *From Interstate 295, take the Westampton exit 45A. Travel east on County Road 626 (Rancocas Road) for 1.7 miles to the entrance on the right.*

Ownership: New Jersey Audubon Society (609) 261-2495

Size: 120 acres   **Closest Town:** Mount Holly

Description: A corridor, or greenway, along the Cooper River, Greenwald Memorial and Pennypacker parks are rich with history as well as wildlife. The remains of the first complete dinosaur skeleton were unearthed in 1858 in an area which is now part of the park. *Hadrosaurus foulkii* is now the New Jersey State Dinosaur. These parks are an oasis in a busy suburban area.

Viewing Information: At Greenwald Memorial Park, which lies within Pennypacker Park, an easy walking route extends for more than a mile along the Cooper River from busy King's Highway (New Jersey 41) west along Park Boulevard to the park system office. Early morning is the best time to see birds here, especially during the spring migration, when the trees are alive with warblers and other songbirds but are not yet fully leafed-out. During the summer, visit Hopkins Pond and the surrounding mature hardwood forest (continue south on New Jersey 41 to Hopkins Lane, turn right, and park in parking areas in 0.1 mile) for glimpses of herons, osprey, turtles, raccoons, and opossums.

Other Camden County parks to visit are Berlin Park and New Brooklyn Park. The Camden County Environmental Studies Center is in Berlin Park, along with 5 miles of hiking trails through lowland woods along the Great Egg Harbor River. New Brooklyn Park is an unimproved park surrounding New Brooklyn Lake. Call (609) 795-7275 for information.

Directions: *Greenwald Memorial Park: From New Jersey 70 in Cherry Hill, take New Jersey 41 south for 0.9 mile. Turn right onto Park Boulevard. Park in any of the designated parking areas within the next 1.3 miles. Berlin Park: From New Jersey 30 in Berlin, go south on Broad Street for three blocks. Park entrance is straight ahead.*

Ownership: Camden County Park System (609) 795-7275

Size: Greenwald Memorial Park 47 acres, Pennypacker Park 32 acres, Berlin Park 140 acres

Closest Towns: Haddonfield and Cherry Hill

Famed as a mimic, the mockingbird can imitate many songs and sounds. The mockingbird shows partiality to living in suburban/urban areas where it is well known for its fierce territorial displays. CLAY MYERS

Description: Within the most densely populated municipality of Gloucester County, there is a rare bit of open space. A portion of the park is dedicated to recreational fields, but there are also hardwood forests, grassy fields, and wetlands for wildlife and wildlife-watchers. The natural vegetation of the area is typical of the transition between inner coastal plain and outer coastal plain.

Viewing Information: Drive to parking lot D to look at the trail map in the office or on the kiosk. Several trails wind around the park. The nature trail is accessed across the road from the office. It winds down to a small stream, crosses a hardwood swamp via a boardwalk, travels up into an oak forest, and across an old farm field. The trail ends with a trip through more wetlands and a holly and tulip poplar forest. Another trail goes through woods and around a pond.

Look for gray and red squirrels, white-tailed deer, red foxes, muskrats, and woodchucks year-round. Canada geese, mallards, great blue herons, red-tailed hawks, turkey vultures, woodpeckers, and the songbirds typical of eastern backyards are common. In the summer, look for little brown bats, green herons, broad-winged hawks, barn swallows, brown thrashers, white-eyed vireos, eastern bluebirds, eastern box turtles, eastern painted turtles, rough green snakes, and green frogs.

Directions: From the junction of New Jersey 47 and County Route 651 (Greentree Road) in Glassboro, travel north on CR 651 for 2.2 miles to the park entrance.

Ownership: Washington Township (609) 589-6427

Size: 300 acres   **Closest Town:** Turnersville, Washington Township

Flying squirrels are nocturnal and almost never venture onto the ground. For these reasons they are difficult to see. Look for them at night in wooded areas close to water, gliding from tree to tree. RAY DAVIS

LOWER DELAWARE RIVER

123

65. FORT MOTT STATE PARK

Description: Fort Mott State Park is on the estuary of the Delaware River. Fort Mott was built during the 19th century to protect the coastline during wartime and remnants of its battlements remain visible. Across the river in Delaware is the aptly named Fort Delaware. However, if you want to step into Delaware without crossing the river, just walk north of the state park to a little piece of land that is legally in Delaware. Nearby Supawna Meadows NWR is a wetlands restoration area.

Viewing Information: Walk right to the edge of the river or along the top of the main battery for a view of the surrounding region. During spring migration, you may find horseshoe crabs and shorebirds along the shoreline, especially at low tide. From the seawall and pier, you can see fish and invertebrates in the Delaware River. Although the salinity of the river varies with the season and amount of rain, this is a tidal area. In the spring, summer, and fall, egrets and herons nest on Pea Patch Island in Delaware and fly back and forth across the river to feed. During fall migration and in the winter, look for snow geese and Canada geese. White-tailed deer come to the river to drink, but you will probably just see their tracks.

Directions: *From New Jersey 49 in Salem, travel west on NJ 49 for approximately 3 miles to Lighthouse Road. Turn left and travel 4 miles into the park.*

Ownership: NJDEP Division of Parks and Forestry (609) 935-3218

Size: 104 acres   **Closest Town:** Salem

The Peapatch Island heronry, located in the Delaware River between Delaware City, Delaware, and Ft. Mott, New Jersey, is the largest Atlantic Coast rookery north of Florida. Nine species of herons nest here. JOHN AND KAREN HOLLINGSWORTH

66. SALEM RIVER WILDLIFE MANAGEMENT AREA

Description: Known locally as Mannington marsh or meadows, much of the marsh was impounded for agricultural purposes back in the 1700s and remains so today. The rest of the marsh is tidal and, being in the upper reaches of the Delaware estuary, flows with brackish water. The WMA is made up of several old farms, and some of the walking trails follow former nursery roads. Look around for trees in unusual groupings. These are nursery stock that have grown wild and now provides valuable habitat for songbirds in migration.

Viewing Information: A good view of the marsh is just south of the parking area on New Jersey 45. A trail from the parking lot takes you to an elevated platform at the edge of the marsh. Fall and winter birding is excellent when the pickerelweed, spatterdock, and American lotus die down, making it much easier to see the rafts of ducks. Look for northern pintails, gadwalls, and green-winged teal. Thousands of Canada geese and snow geese feed in the nearby farm fields during the fall and winter. Nesting birds in the marsh include American coots, mute swans, and an abundance of red-winged blackbirds. During spring and fall migration, look for warblers and other songbirds from the trail that loops to and from the parking area. Summer residents include yellow warblers and common yellowthroats.

Salem River WMA is a natural area with no facilities. OPEN FOR HUNTING DURING PRESCRIBED SEASONS.

Directions: *From U.S. Highway 40 and New Jersey 45, drive 4.3 miles south on NJ 45 to WMA sign on the right (west) side of the road. Pull in to park. Or, for other views of the marsh, continue 1.8 miles south on NJ 45 to first right turn (Bypass Road). Go 0.1 mile and turn right onto County Route 620. Travel 1.6 miles to the overlook. To continue from the overlook, turn left onto Nimrod Road and travel 1.8 miles to County Route 540. Turn left again and travel 1.8 miles back to NJ 45, stopping for views along the way. Please obey No Parking and posted signs in these locations: they are outside the WMA.*

Ownership: NJDEP, Division of Fish, Game and Wildlife (609) 629-0090

Size: 1,121 acres   **Closest Town:** Salem

This northern pintail is just one of the many species of waterfowl that congregate in large numbers at the Salem River WMA in winter. There are few places in New Jersey that rival the winter waterfowl viewing opportunities that exist at Salem River.
PAUL M. CASTELLI

LOWER DELAWARE RIVER

125

67. ABBOTTS MEADOW WILDLIFE MANAGEMENT AREA

Description: This boundary area has upland fields, meadows, and pastures separated by hedgerows. The several species of sparrows you are likely to see in the pastures give the area an outstanding reputation for birding.

Viewing Information: Travel along Money Island Road slowly, using your car as a bird blind, and scan the bushes of the hedgerows on both sides. Park in the area at the end of the road and either walk the road again or take the footpath out to some of the hummocks. These hummocks, or small islands, are rarely more than a foot higher than surrounding elevations, but the height allows cedar trees, shrubs, and vines to grow. The high tension wires from the power plant offer roosting places for black vultures, turkey vultures, and ospreys nesting in the area. Abbots Meadow WMA is a natural area with no facilities. OPEN FOR HUNTING DURING PRESCRIBED SEASONS.

Directions: *Take New Jersey 49 east 0.7 mile from its intersection with New Jersey 45 to County Route 658. Turn right onto CR 658 (Hancock's Bridge Road) at the sign for Hancock's Bridge. Travel approximately 3 miles and turn right onto CR 624 (Fort Elfsborg Road). Proceed for 2 miles to Money Island Road and turn left. The parking area is at the end of the Money Island Road in 1 mile.*

Ownership: NJDEP, Division of Fish, Game, and Wildlife (609) 629-0090

Size: 431 acres   **Closest town:** Hancock's Bridge

68. PARVIN STATE PARK

Description: The attractions of Parvin State Park include lakes, forests, natural areas, hiking trails, a nature center, and campsites, all within 6 miles of the sprawling city of Vineland. Cabins are available from April 1 to October 31. Park naturalists offer regularly scheduled programs.

Viewing Information: At least 136 species of bird travel through or reside in the park. The quiet observer may find white-tailed deer, white-footed mice, and river otters. Frogs, salamanders, toads, turtles, and nonvenomous snakes also inhabit the park. The naturalist's choice of trails includes the Thundergust Lake Trail, about 1 mile long, and the connecting Long Trail, which covers more than 5 miles. Trail guides are available at the office.

Directions: *From Exit 35 on New Jersey 55, take Garden Road toward Brotmanville. Travel 0.7 mile to Gershel Avenue. Turn left and, after 1.7 miles, turn right onto County Route 540. Follow CR 540 for 2.4 miles to the park entrance, and travel an additional 0.3 mile to reach the park office.*

Ownership: NJDEP Division of Parks and Forestry (609) 358-8616

Size: 1,135 acres   **Closest towns:** Norma and Centerton

CAPE MAY–DELAWARE BAY REGION

Sandy and flat, the Cape May–Delaware Bay Region is part of the outer coastal plain. Bordered on the east by the Atlantic Ocean and on the west by Delaware Bay, the region boasts some of the best bird watching in the state. The funnel-like shape of the Cape May Peninsula acts to concentrate birds as they migrate down the Atlantic coast. Many species of birds rest and refuel here before and after crossing the Delaware Bay during spring and fall migration. Breeding birds are abundant and include many endangered species such as the bald eagle and black rail.

Because federal and state agencies and nonprofit conservation organizations own a large percentage of the land, the Delaware Bayshore has the lowest population density in New Jersey. The high concentration of rare and endangered plants and animals in this area is due to the lack of development. In fact, the endangered tiger salamander and southern gray tree frog live only in this region in New Jersey.

One of the few places in the world you can find joint vetch, a twining plant, is along the wild and scenic Maurice River. The state's largest native stands of wild rice grow along the river banks, and Atlantic white cedars line the stream corridors and bogs. The large tracts of southern hardwood and pine-oak forests covering the region's interior provide some of the best habitat in the state for forest-dependent species like the barred owl, red-shouldered hawk, and the hundreds of songbirds that nest here and winter in the tropics.

Salt marshes border the region, forming where shallow ocean or bay waters

meet gently sloping, sheltered coastlines. This occurs on the east coast behind barrier islands and on the west coast in sheltered bay coves. The salt marsh acts as a "breadbasket," producing nearly 10 tons of organic matter per acre per year. This organic matter forms the basis of a food web which affects species that live both in and out of the salt marsh, including humans. Fresh food and nutrients flow into tidal creeks with the tides twice daily, providing ample food for the creatures who live in or near the marsh.

This is an agricultural area as well, producing lettuce, peppers, tomatoes, cabbages, and soybeans. Large wholesale nurseries and smaller garden centers supplement the region's agriculture, giving credence to New Jersey's nickname "The Garden State." Traditional local industries in the past included boat building, fishing, and oystering. In the early 1900s, Bivalve was the oyster capital of the world. The fish and shellfish industries have declined since the 1950s, but the state's remnant oyster fleet still sit at the docks in the towns of Bivalve and Shellpile. Major industries in the area today are sand mining and glass manufacturing. Sand mining operations leave large deep lakes often surrounded by sandy beaches, which are used by beach-nesting birds.

Fortunately, much of this region has retained its rural flavor. The abundance of federal, state, and nonprofit lands has played an important role in maintaining the ecological integrity of this region.

Above: *All marine reptiles, such as this loggerhead turtle, found in American waters are protected by the Federal Endangered Species Act of 1973. Overharvest and loss of critical nesting habitat are largely responsible for species decline.* HERB SEGARS

Preceding page: *Snow geese begin arriving along the bayshore in late October. Huge flocks of several thousand birds forming long, ragged Vs are a frequent fall sight.* JEFF LEPORE

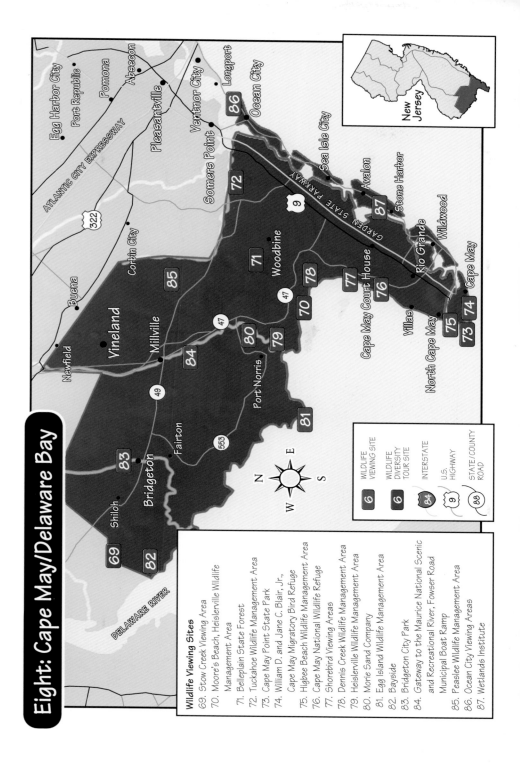

Eight: Cape May/Delaware Bay

Wildlife Viewing Sites

69. Stow Creek Viewing Area
70. Moore's Beach, Heislerville Wildlife Management Area
71. Belleplain State Forest
72. Tuckahoe Wildlife Management Area
73. Cape May Point State Park
74. William D. and Jane C. Blair, Jr., Cape May Migratory Bird Refuge
75. Higbee Beach Wildlife Management Area
76. Cape May National Wildlife Refuge
77. Shorebird Viewing Areas
78. Dennis Creek Wildlife Management Area
79. Heislerville Wildlife Management Area
80. Morie Sand Company
81. Egg Island Wildlife Management Area
82. Bayside
83. Bridgeton City Park
84. Gateway to the Maurice National Scenic and Recreational River, Fowser Road Municipal Boat Ramp
85. Peaslee Wildlife Management Area
86. Ocean City Viewing Areas
87. Wetlands Institute

New Jersey

Legend

- WILDLIFE VIEWING SITE
- WILDLIFE DIVERSITY TOUR SITE
- INTERSTATE
- U.S. HIGHWAY
- STATE/COUNTY ROAD

129

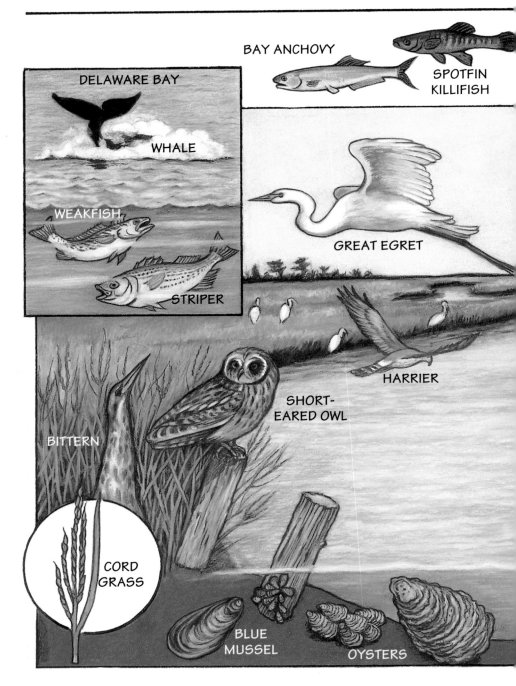

BAY ANCHOVY

SPOTFIN KILLIFISH

DELAWARE BAY

WHALE

WEAKFISH

STRIPER

GREAT EGRET

HARRIER

SHORT-EARED OWL

BITTERN

CORD GRASS

BLUE MUSSEL

OYSTERS

   The Cape May–Delaware Bay Region is surrounded by salt marsh, one of the most productive habitats on earth. These marshes act as nurseries, wave buffers, water purifiers, oxygen pumps, and food pantries for a menagerie of wildlife. The marshes provide crucial habitat for spectacular numbers of breeding and migrating ducks, geese, herons, egrets, wading birds, shorebirds, and raptors. Shallow bay coves and tidal creeks serve as nurseries and foraging grounds for a variety of

BLACK DRUM

BALD EAGLE

RED KNOTS EATING HORSESHOE CRAB EGGS

RED-WINGED BLACKBIRD

BLACK-CROWNED NIGHT HERON

CLAPPER RAIL AND NEST

GLASS EEL

EEL GRASS

BAY SCALLOP

FIDDLER CRAB

FLOUNDER

migratory fish. The Bayshore is the site of one of New Jersey's most spectacular wildlife phenomenon: it hosts the largest concentration of shorebirds in the western hemisphere during spring migration. The birds stop to gorge themselves on horseshoe crab eggs before resuming their 10,000-mile trip to Arctic breeding grounds. In addition, the extensive woodlands and hardwood swamps are extremely important for songbirds and raptors. Many of New Jersey's bald eagles nest here.

69. STOW CREEK VIEWING AREA

Description: Bald eagles are making a comeback in southern New Jersey and this site may provide the best opportunity to see nesting eagles. A large old sycamore stands next to an abandoned farmhouse at the edge of Stow Creek, providing a scenic location for this seven-year-old eagle nest. However, in 1997 the nest failed, and the cause of the failure has never been determined. Often, after a failure, eagles will abandon a nesting site. As of the publication of this guide in January of 1998, the eagles were working on the nest. If they choose to remain and nest this year, biologists will place eagle chicks in the nest for the adults to raise. This action will help ensure the success of the nest. The site also provides plenty of opportunities to see nesting osprey, and a variety of wading birds and marsh wildlife species. The status of the eagle nest can be obtained by calling (609) 628-2103.

Diversity Tour Information: At the Stow Creek viewing area DFGW/ENSP biologists work in cooperation with the private landowner to protect the nest of a pair of bald eagles. The nest, roughly 7 feet in diameter by 4.5 feet deep, has been the home of 16 young eagles since 1990. Bald eagles are very sensitive to human disturbance, however, and will abandon their nest sites if people encroach too closely during nesting. For this reason, all viewing must be from the shoulder of New Bridge Road or the observation deck on the west side of the creek.

Nesting bald eagles reside in New Jersey year-round, usually remaining in the area of their nests. Eagles generally build their large stick nests near water, in trees taller than the forest canopy. They begin courtship and nest building in early January, adding new material to their existing nest. Pairs lay one to three eggs in mid-February to early March, which incubate for about 35 days. Upon hatching, the chicks are helpless and require close parental care. After about five weeks the young birds begin to stand up and feed themselves when the adults deliver food. Young birds are fledged at about 11 weeks of age, usually in early July. Adults continue to feed the young near the nest for several weeks while the young learn the rudiments of flying. In late August, young eagles leave the area as they learn to hunt and soar. Many juveniles spend the following winter in the Chesapeake Bay area, where there is open water and abundant food.

The bald eagle is New Jersey's largest and best-known raptor. It is also an indicator of environmental health. Since the eagle is at the top of the food chain, it is more adversely affected by the presence of dangerous chemicals in its environment than the animals it feeds on. The pesticide DDT was a major factor in the eagle's population decline from the 1950s through the 1970s. Prior to 1960, there were 22 nesting pairs in the state, but by 1970 the population had dwindled to just one nest.

However, the ban on DDT in 1972 set the stage for the eagles' recovery. From 1982 to 1990, DFGW/ENSP biologists raised and released 60 eaglets along the Delaware Bayshore and Atlantic Coast. This project bolstered the population of bald eagles in New Jersey to 14 nesting pairs in 1997. The Bald Eagle Restoration Program is funded by the "Check-off for Wildlife" box on the NJ State Income Tax Form and the sale of New Jersey's Conserve Wildlife license plates.

In addition to the eagle viewing opportunities, Stow Creek is a good place to study a salt marsh. Upstream and inland from here, the creek is all fresh water; however, from this point south to the Delaware Bay the water is salty.

All marsh life is adapted to feed, move, rest, and nest in rhythm with the tides. Some snails and insects climb the cordgrass twice each day to stay ahead of the rising tides. Look for wrens and swallows that feed on these climbers. In addition to the nesting osprey, other birds that you may see feeding in the tidal marsh include snowy egrets, green-backed and great blue herons, Canada geese, and mallards. Spring and fall are good times to visit this brackish, tidal marsh. Stow Creek viewing area is a natural area with no facilities.

Directions: *From the junction of New Jersey 49 and New Jersey 45 in Salem, travel 0.7 mile east on NJ 49 to County Route 658. Turn right onto CR 658 (Hancock's Bridge Road) at the sign for Hancock's Bridge. CR 658 makes a left turn onto Grieve's Parkway in 0.3 mile. Turn right onto CR 623 (New Bridge Road) and travel about 8 miles to the parking area on the right (south) side of the road, just before the bridge over Stow Creek.*

Wildlife Diversity Tour Directions:

FROM STOW CREEK (SITE 69) TO MOORE'S BEACH WMA (SITE 70)

From Stow Creek viewing area, continue south on County Route 623 into the historic town of Greenwich. Turn left onto County Route 607 in the center of town and proceed approximately 5 miles to the intersection of New Jersey 49 in Bridgeton. Turn right and take NJ 49 east to the town of Millville. Watch carefully for the junction of NJ 49 and New Jersey 47 in Millville. Turn right and follow NJ 47 (Delsea Drive) south for approximately 13 miles to Moores Beach Road. Turn right and proceed 0.5 mile to parking area.

Ownership: NJDEP, Division of Fish, Game, and Wildlife (609) 628-2103

Size: About 30 acres   **Closest Town:** Canton, Lower Alloways Creek Township

The best opportunity for viewing nesting bald eagles in New Jersey is at the Stow Creek viewing area. This nest is one of about 15 eagle nests in the state that have been established after an extensive restoration project carried out by the Endangered and Nongame Species Program. LEN RUE, JR.

70. MOORE'S BEACH–HEISLERVILLE WILDLIFE MANAGEMENT AREA

Description: Delaware Bay is the premier resting and feeding site for hundreds of thousands of shorebirds during their spring migration, attracted by eggs laid by the world's largest concentration of breeding horseshoe crabs. Although this spring spectacle is short lived, the beauty of the salt marsh at Moore's Beach can be enjoyed in any season. For your own comfort, avoid calm days during the biting-fly season in midsummer.

Diversity Tour Information: Delaware Bay is the largest oil transfer port on the East Coast, and a thoroughfare for thousands of vessels carrying essential goods to the ports of Camden, Wilmington, and Philadelphia. Its location, midway between shorebird wintering grounds of South America and the nesting grounds of the Arctic, also make it a thoroughfare for thousands of birds. Bay beaches and salt marshes are feeding and resting areas for shorebird species such as sanderlings, red knots, ruddy turnstones, and semipalmated sandpipers. Many of these birds fly nonstop for four days from South America to Delaware Bay. Moore's Beach is one of about six bay beaches to host a large portion of the Western Hemisphere's migrating shorebird species. All told, nearly a million shorebirds pour into Delaware Bay each spring from about May 13 to June 6.

Delaware Bay beaches are also essential for spawning horseshoe crabs. In May and June, thousands of horseshoe crabs crowd the beaches to mate and lay their eggs. Horseshoe crabs are found from Maine to Florida, but more of

Delaware Bay is the most important horseshoe crab breeding location in the world. For eons, the fat-rich eggs deposited in the sand by the crabs has fueled the northward migration of nearly a million shorebirds that make a two-week stop on their 3,000-mile flight to the Arctic. BRECK P. KENT

them nest on the sandy beaches of the lower Delaware Bay than anywhere else. The female, larger than the male, digs a hole in the sand at the water's edge and deposits thousands of green pinhead-sized eggs which hatch in 4 to 6 weeks.

The thousands of shorebirds that arrive shortly after the crabs start spawning feast on the profusion of readily available eggs. Shorebirds gorge themselves on these eggs, doubling their arrival weight in about two weeks. It is estimated that the total pool of shorebirds moving through Delaware Bay each spring will consume over 300 tons of the tiny horseshoe crab eggs! This feast fuels the second leg of the shorebirds' journey to their Arctic nesting areas.

In addition to the crabs and shorebirds, there is plenty to see year-round at this interesting viewing site.

Watch for marsh hawks, egrets, great blue herons, northern diamondback terrapins, and marsh wrens. Viewing is particularly good from spring through fall. At low tide, clapper rails are easy to spot digging for invertebrates in the creeks. In winter, look for snow geese feeding in the marsh. Northern harriers and red-tailed hawks hover and soar over the marsh in search of prey. The salt marshes and mud flats also hold black-bellied plovers, dunlin, and thousands of dowitchers. In the summer look for egrets, glossy ibis, nesting seaside sparrows, and willets. From the beach, look for scoters and other bay ducks in the winter and early spring. Even white pelicans and ruffs have been sighted here before!

An active peregrine falcon nesting tower maintained by the DFGW/ENSP is located to the west of the road. Although coastal marshes are not considered typical nesting habitat for peregrines, an abundant prey base and freedom from predation by great horned owls made Delaware Bay sites a good place to reintroduce this endangered species. The peregrine completely vanished from the eastern part of the United States in the mid-1960s as a result of toxins like

Hunted nearly to extinction in the early 1900s by plume hunters, the snowy egret is now a common sight in New Jersey marshes. CLAY MYERS

DDT in the food chain. Beginning in 1975, DFGW/ENSP biologists released young captive-bred falcons at this and other areas along the coast, and today about 15 pair of peregrines nest each year in New Jersey.

Rising water levels and erosion have destroyed the beachfront development that existed at Moore's Beach. Erosion of dunes is caused by a decrease in the natural vegetation that help hold dunes in place and by high water levels during and after storms. In addition, overall water levels throughout the Delaware Bay and Atlantic Ocean are rising slightly each year due to increased runoff from the North American continent. Depending on the tide, you may be able to see former streets that have been overtaken by the bay. Storm flooding and the surging tide continue to threaten the access road. However, these changes are actually bringing about improvements in wildlife habitat by reclaiming the waterfront and restoring tidal flow to the marshes that were formerly diked for salt hay farming.

DO NOT WALK ON THE BEACH OR ALLOW PETS TO RUN ON THE BEACH WHEN SHOREBIRDS ARE PRESENT IN THE SPRING.

OPEN FOR HUNTING DURING PRESCRIBED SEASON.

Directions: *From the southern end of New Jersey 55 and its intersection with New Jersey 47, continue almost 8.5 miles south on NJ 47. Turn right onto Moore's Beach Road and proceed to parking area.*

Wildlife Diversity Tour Directions:

FROM MOORE'S BEACH WMA (SITE 70) TO BELLEPLAIN STATE FOREST (SITE 71)

From Moore's Beach WMA, return to New Jersey 47, turn right (south), and drive for 0.2 mile. Turn left onto Hands Mill Road (CR 651). Proceed on Hands Mill Road (which becomes spur 550 at the first crossroads) for approximately 7 miles to where it joins CR 550. Turn right onto Woodbine Avenue (CR 550) in Belleplain and travel 3.4 miles to Belleplain State Forest entrance on the right.

Ownership: NJDEP, Division of Fish, Game, and Wildlife (609) 628-2436

Size: Part of Heislerville Wildlife Management Area

Closest Town: Delmont, Maurice River Township

A large percentage of the East Coast's shorebird population would be lost if Delaware Bay's horseshoe crab population were overharvested. The fat-rich horseshoe crab eggs are the only food source that gives the birds enough fat reserves to complete their flight to their Arctic breeding grounds.

71. BELLEPLAIN STATE FOREST

Description: Belleplain State Forest has miles of marked trails and unimproved roads suitable for hiking, horseback riding, cross-country skiing, and wildlife watching. American holly trees and mountain laurel grow along the roadsides, and Atlantic white cedar swamps dot the lowlands around the waterways. Lake Nummy and the nearby nature center are available for a number of recreational activities and programs, respectively.

Diversity Tour Information: The Belleplain State Forest, lying within the Pinelands National Reserve, contains the greatest variety of habitats anywhere in New Jersey, including saltwater marsh, Atlantic white cedar swamp, mixed hardwood swamp, and oak-hickory forest. In the spring and fall, migrating songbirds such as blue-winged warblers, scarlet tanagers, and prothonotary warblers make the forest sparkle with color.

Belleplain contains one of the only oak-hickory forests in south Jersey. The southern portion of the forest is a beautiful illustration of this biotic community. Food and shelter for wildlife are abundant in oak-hickory forests: acorns and hickory nuts offer valuable nutrition and require only a small outlay of foraging energy. In the summer, oaks and hickories sprout from their stumps, placing succulent leaves within easy reach of animals. When leaves fall, they decay slowly because of the tannin in their cells, creating a thick batting of leaves for small rodents, reptiles, and amphibians—including spotted and marbled salamanders, five-lined skinks, eastern box turtles, and the red-backed vole—for burrowing and foraging.

One of the best ways to see the forest is to drive south on New Jersey 47 to Jakes Landing Road. Turn right on Jakes Landing Road and right again onto Beaver Causeway Road (if you follow Beaver Causeway to its end you will be

Listen for the tap, tap, tapping of woodpeckers as they search for insects on dead and dying trees. Dead trees also provide nesting habitat for these cavity nesters.
DONNA L. BLASZCAK

back out on NJ 47). This road leads not only to upland hardwood forests, but also through a white cedar swamp. The continuous forest cover is important habitat to many neotropical migratory birds, such as cerulean warblers and ovenbirds, as well as for interior-forest raptor species such as red-shouldered hawks and barred owls. On the edge of the forest look for black and white warblers and red-tailed hawks.

Along Beaver Causeway, you will see the remnants of three old plantations of white pine. Members of the old Civilian Conservation Corps planted these pine stands in the 1930s. Over time some of the old pine trees have died and fallen to the forest floor to decay. The process provides food and shelter for species like red-backed salamanders that seek cool, damp habitats.

If you continue south on Jakes Landing Road (instead of turning onto Beaver Causeway) you will enter the Dennis Creek Wildlife Management Area, an interesting transition zone between upland hardwood forests and a typical Delaware Bay marshland ecosystem. Dennis Creek WMA is a viewing area described later in this region. In addition to excellent marshland habitats and a good opportunity to view many hawks, songbirds, and owls, there is access to the Delaware Bay by way of a boat ramp into Dennis Creek.

Another good way to see the forest is to walk the 1.5-mile, self-guided trail around Lake Nummy or the 6.5 mile trail connecting Lake Nummy to East Creek Pond. Look for signs of white-tailed deer, red foxes, raccoons, Virginia opossums, red, gray, and flying squirrels, muskrats, and beavers. Also look for Cooper's and broad-winged hawks, blue-gray gnatcatchers, red-eyed vireos, scarlet tanagers, and several varieties of woodpeckers.

Early to mid-September is the peak of the flight for Cooper's hawks. Forested areas and shrubby fields provide critical resting and feeding areas for these endangered hawks. ARTHUR M. PANZER

Elsewhere in Belleplain, biotic succession, a natural event in a normal ecosystem, is being dramatically accelerated by gypsy moths. Gypsy moths, an introduced species of leaf-eaters, have infested south Jersey's forests off and on since the 1970s. However, most defoliation has not been so severe or as frequent as at Belleplain. The repeated defoliation of many white, red, and black oaks by the gypsy moths has killed some trees. Forest managers have salvaged some of the dying oaks for use as firewood, while other dead trees are left standing to provide vertical habitat. Some animals use the cavities in these trees for nests, others feed off of the insects that live in and on the dead wood, and still others use the trees as roosts or perches. Look for cavity dwellers like flying squirrels, raccoons, Virginia opossums, pileated and red-bellied woodpeckers, and tufted titmice.

The forests along the Belleplain-Woodbine Road (County Route 550) are a good place to look at the dead and dying oak forests. Note the massive amounts of regrowth in the understory of white pines, red cedars, and maples. These early successional tree species are shade intolerant and would not have been able to grow here if it were not for the death of the oaks. More shade tolerant hardwood species will eventually replace this new community of sun-loving species. These "seres," or stages, are all part of a predictable pattern of succession, and an equally predictable group of wildlife species can be expected to appear within each sere. Maps and trail guides are available at the office. OPEN FOR HUNTING IN PRESCRIBED AREAS.

Directions: From U.S. Highway 9 in Oceanview, take County Route 550 west for about 8 miles to state forest office, following Belleplain State Forest signs.

Wildlife Diversity Tour Directions:

FROM BELLEPLAIN STATE FOREST (SITE 71) TO TUCKAHOE WMA (SITE 72)

From Belleplain State Forest Office return to CR 550 and turn right, east. Take CR 550 into the town of Woodbine. Turn left onto CR 550/557. Continue straight on CR 557 and proceed for several miles into the town of Tuckahoe. Turn right onto NJ 50 and proceed for 2 miles to traffic light. Turn left at the light onto CR 631 and proceed for 0.3 miles to the entrance to Tuckahoe WMA on the left.

Ownership: NJDEP, Division of Parks and Forestry (609) 861-2404

Size: 12,120 acres **Closest Town:** Woodbine

Deep forest birds are suffering from the destruction of breeding, nesting, and wintering habitat through forest fragmentation—the breaking up of forests into small parcels. The large, contiguous coastal plain forest at Belleplain is critical for the survival of woodland species like barred owls, red-shouldered hawks, numerous warblers, and songbirds.

Description: The scenic Tuckahoe River winds its way to the Great Egg Harbor River and Bay through an expanse of salt marsh and tidal creeks. Birdwatching is good here, as it is along the six brackish water impoundments on the upland edges of the tract. Located on the edge of the Pinelands, the woodlands bordering the salt marsh are a mixture of pine and oak trees. A hardwood swamp and small freshwater lake provide additional habitat for beaver, turtles, frogs, and fish.

Diversity Tour Information: The Corbin City area offers an 8-mile drive on a sand and gravel road that runs between three large impoundments and the salt marsh and ends by going through a stretch of pine-oak forest. You can drive the entire route or use the pull-outs for a chance to walk the sand trails and look out over the impoundments and salt marsh. If you prefer viewing wildlife on foot, start your visit on the Tuckahoe side of the river. Here, you must park your car and walk the sand trails along the impoundments. You will find similar wildlife in both areas.

Facing the salt marsh, look for wildlife activity at the "ecotone," or edge, formed between the marsh and adjacent tidal creek. One key to wildlife activity in the ecotone is the abundant supply of food that arrives twice daily on the rising tide. The tall salt marsh cordgrass along the creek banks provides shelter for wary birds, like rails, who search the exposed mud for invertebrates. Sora, black, clapper, and Virginia rails all live here, and you may see an otter swimming in the tidal creeks in search of fish.

During spring and fall migrations, scan the exposed mud flats of the tidal creeks and impoundments at low tide for shorebirds like sandpipers, plovers, and yellowlegs probing the mud for invertebrates. Muskrats, willets, egrets,

An uncommon sight in the eastern United States, golden eagles are often sighted at Tuckahoe during the eagle census conducted in January. CHARLES H. WILLEY

and herons can be seen year-round, and American bitterns and mink are present but elusive. Bald eagles nest nearby and are sometimes seen fishing over or resting near the impoundments. Waterfowl such as hooded mergansers, blue and green-winged teal, northern pintails, gadwalls, and American wigeons congregate on the impoundments during migration.

A growing problem throughout the world is the invasion of natural ecosystems by non-native plant and animal species referred to as "exotics." The beautiful mute swans seen in the impoundments are a good example of invasion by a non-native species, which are not native to this ecosystem, or even to North America. Although beautiful, the swans have a negative impact on native ducks and geese by competing aggressively for nesting territory. If the swans were not present, more species of nesting waterfowl would most likely live here. Exotics represent a serious threat to biodiversity by competing with native species for food, water, and space, and in some instances, have caused native species to become endangered.

The impoundments at Corbin City and Tuckahoe were created in the late 1940s and early 1950s to attract a greater diversity and abundance of wildlife than would normally be found on the same acreage of salt marsh. The impoundments are an example of the habitat creation and management that is carried out by the NJDEP/DFGW on wildlife management areas like this one throughout the state. Today, NJDEP/DFGW biologists are doing experimental water level management in one impoundment. This effort is intended to help establish a new aquatic plant community that will be an important new food sources for migratory waterfowl and will also maximize the feeding area for migrating shorebirds by increasing mud flat exposure times.

Tuckahoe WMA is a natural area with no facilities. OPEN FOR HUNTING DURING PRESCRIBED SEASONS.

Directions: *From the junction of U.S. Highway 9 and New Jersey 50 in Seaville, take NJ 50 north for 4.8 miles to County Route 631. Turn right and travel 0.3 mile to WMA entrance on the left. Turn left onto the sand and gravel road and travel 0.5 mile to the office on the right. Stop at the office for information and maps. To go to Corbin City, continue north on NJ 50 for 3 miles to Griscom Mill Road. Turn right. The road turns to sand and gravel and continues for 8 miles past the impoundments before it intersects again with NJ 50 as Gibson Creek Road.*

Wildlife Diversity Tour Directions:

FROM TUCKAHOE WMA (SITE 72) TO CAPE MAY POINT STATE PARK (SITE 73)

From anywhere within the Tuckahoe WMA, return to New Jersey 50 and travel south to its end at Garden State Parkway interchange 20. Take the Garden State Parkway to its end in the historic town of Cape May. Continue straight on what is now Laffayette Street (County Route 633). Turn right onto Sunset Boulevard (CR 606) and travel 2 miles to Cape May Point. Turn left onto Lighthouse Avenue and follow the signs for Cape May Point State Park. Entrance will be on the left.

Ownership: NJDEP, Division of Fish, Game, and Wildlife (609) 628-2436

Size: 13,742 acres   **Closest Towns:** Tuckahoe and Corbin City

Description: A 157-foot tall lighthouse, which dominates the park, is a contemporary reminder of New Jersey's maritime heritage. Nearby, an observation platform known as the "Hawk Watch," provides excellent views of a freshwater pond, marsh, and migrating hawks in the fall. A large portion of the park is a designated Natural Area and has more than 3 miles of trails and boardwalks for nature study and hiking. There is easy access to the observation platform, trails, and beach from the parking lot. The park has a 0.5-mile, self-guided nature trail that is barrier-free. Visit the museum, visitor center, and environmental education center for a glimpse into the natural history of the area.

Diversity Tour Information: The "Hawk Watch" observation platform provides a bird's-eye view of one of the nation's most extraordinary autumn hawk migrations. Beginning in September and extending through December, tens of thousands of raptors, including bald eagles, peregrine falcons, ospreys, goshawks, Cooper's hawks, and various species of owl pass the platform on the Point. New Jersey Audubon's Cape May Bird Observatory volunteers and staff provide informative programs for visitors throughout the fall.

The Cape May peninsula has become world renowned for its importance to migratory birds. The peninsula acts as a funnel for songbirds, shorebirds, waterfowl, butterflies, and hawks migrating along the Atlantic Flyway. Undeveloped habitats on Cape May are critical staging areas that provide important resting and feeding opportunities for migrating birds as they prepare for their arduous journey across the Delaware Bay. The park's shrubs, trees, and weeds

Dragonflies are a common sight during the fall migration at Cape May Point. This tenspot skimmer is a common dragonfly found near most bodies of shallow water. Dragonflies are fierce predators on other insects and catch them with amazing aerial acrobatics. CLAY MYERS

come alive with songbirds gleaning insects, seeds, and fruits to fuel their migration, and hawks perform aerial acrobatics to pursue them. This scenario is repeated thousands of times, everywhere on the Cape where housing and commercial development have not replaced natural habitats.

A recent study conducted by DFGW/ENSP biologists revealed that 40 percent of the habitat available to migrating birds on Cape May, as recently as 1985, has now been developed. There is growing concern about the amount of habitat lost to development on the peninsula. DFGW/ENSP has initiated a habitat conservation strategy that is intended to help landowners, regulators, and planners agree on which habitats must be preserved to support migratory wildlife. The New Jersey Audubon Society, The Nature Conservancy, and the New Jersey Association of Environmental Commissions are working in partnership with DFGW/ENSP on this long-term conservation strategy.

A short drive to Higbee Beach Wildlife Management Area, which is described later in this section, rewards visitors with glimpses of hundreds of species of migrating songbirds and hawks. Higbee Beach is managed specifically to provide habitat for migratory wildlife.

At Higbee Beach you will see that birds are not the only migrants to pass through Cape May. Butterflies, particularly monarchs, dragonflies, and damselflies, fill the sky with brilliant colors on their way south. Migrating dragonflies and butterflies also use the peninsula as a resting area. NJDEP/DFGW biologists decided to increase Higbee Beach's butterfly watching opportunities by creating a 30- x 70-foot butterfly garden. A nearby field is also planted with wildflowers. Both the garden and the field provide a concentrated nectar source for butterflies, as well as an excellent place for visitors to view butterflies migrating through the area. The wildflowers planted were chosen for their diversity of color, which helps to attract the butterflies. The butterflies, in turn, pollinate the flowers, ensuring the plants' ability to propagate.

The William D. and Jane C. Blair Cape May Migratory Bird Refuge, which is described later in this section, is also just a short drive from Cape May Point State Park. The refuge provides a haven for two state-listed endangered species: the least tern and the piping plover. These birds spend their winters flying from South Carolina to South America. New Jersey's beaches comprise a significant portion of the entire breeding population's nesting habitat. Therefore, the fate of least terns and piping plovers in New Jersey has worldwide significance. Piping plovers and least terns nest on sand beaches, dunes, or occasionally on sandy gravel or dredge spoil. Their nests are shallow depressions in the sand, frequently lined with clam shell fragments. The nests and chicks are well camouflaged and difficult to see.

Directions: *From Cape May, take County Route 606 (Sunset Boulevard) west toward Cape May Point. Turn left (south) on Lighthouse Avenue. Follow the signs to the state park entrance on your left.*

Ownership: NJDEP, Division of Parks and Forestry (609) 884-2159

Size: 190 acres   **Closest Towns:** Cape May Point, Cape May

74. WILLIAM D. AND JANE C. BLAIR, JR., CAPE MAY MIGRATORY BIRD REFUGE

Description: Recognized as one of the East Coast's premier birding hot spots, fall migration in Cape May is spectacular. Thousands of raptors, shorebirds, songbirds, and waterfowl pass through the refuge on their way south. An observation platform, located 800 feet from the parking lot, overlooks freshwater and brackish wetlands. The beach is an easy 0.3-mile walk from the parking lot. Hiking the 1-mile loop trail takes you through meadows and wetlands, past mud flats, and along the beach front.

Viewing Information: A mile of undeveloped beach front is used by the endangered piping plover and least tern for nesting. Behind the dune, the wetlands offer resting and nesting spots for a variety of other birds. In the fall, look for some of the smaller migrants in addition to raptors and waterfowl. Migrating dragonflies and butterflies, including monarchs on their way to Central America, use the Cape May peninsula as a resting area. Please stay on marked trails, and cross dunes only at crossovers. Nesting birds are vulnerable.

Directions: *Entering Cape May from the Garden State Parkway, continue from the end of the Parkway onto Lafayette Street (County Road 633). At the end of CR 633, take Sunset Boulevard, County Route 606, west. The refuge is within 1 mile, on the left (south) side of the road.*

Ownership: The Nature Conservancy (609) 785-1735

Size: 271 acres   **Closest Towns:** Cape May, Cape May Point

Above: *Piping plovers face many challenges attempting to nest on the New Jersey coast. If the eggs they lay on the beach survive beachgoers, pets, and predators, the chicks are still vulnerable as they cross the open beach to feed at the surf line.*
CLAY MYERS

Opposite: *American beachgrass is one of the few plant species specially adapted to survive the harsh conditions of the dunes. It acts as a dune stabilizer and builder by catching and trapping sand.* DWIGHT HISCANO

145

Description: Higbee Beach is a 1.5-mile stretch of beach containing the last remnant of coastal dune forest on the bayshore. The inland dunes are more than 20 feet high in some places and are stabilized by a forest of holly, red cedar, and beach plum. Several hundred acres of wooded upland with a dense understory, a freshwater marsh, two freshwater ponds, a hardwood swamp, old farm fields, and a coastal dune forest all provide ideal cover for migratory songbirds and raptors. The fields are maintained in early successional vegetation and provide resting and feeding habitat for songbirds and butterflies.

Viewing Information: Birders descend on Higbee Beach in the fall to catch some of the best birding in the world. During fall migration, birds concentrate at the southern tip of Cape May Peninsula, waiting for the best winds to cross the bay. The fall plumage of warblers blends in well with the surroundings here, making birding a challenge. In addition to millions of songbirds, nearly 50,000 raptors migrate down the peninsula every year, and many stop here to rest and feed. A thrilling sight at Higbee is a sharp-shinned, Cooper's, or broad-winged hawk hunting for smaller birds. Approximately 250 bird species are known to use the area at some point during the year. In addition to supporting extensive bird use, the freshwater and upland habitats support a variety of reptiles, amphibians, and butterflies. Look for the endangered eastern tiger salamander and southern gray tree frog.

Higbee Beach WMA is a natural area with no facilities. OPEN FOR HUNTING DURING PRESCRIBED SEASONS.

Directions: *From the end of the Garden State Parkway and its junction with New Jersey 109, take NJ 109 west to its junction with New Jersey 9. Turn left onto NJ 9 (all turns from right lane) and proceed to first traffic light. Turn left onto County Route 626 (Seashore Road). Proceed to New England Road (first right hand turn) and turn right. Follow New England Road for 1 mile to Hidden Valley Ranch parking area on left. Continue 1 mile further to end of New England Road and beach access parking area. Parking areas close to the beach may be closed during the summer season. Call the number listed for parking information.*

Ownership: NJDEP, Division of Fish, Game, and Wildlife (609) 628-2436

Size: 875 acres   **Closest Towns:** Cape May, Cape May Point

The smallest and most common North American falcon, the American kestrel often perches on utility lines, quietly watching for prey. Often groups of 8–10 can be seen during migration.
ARTHUR MORRIS

76. CAPE MAY NATIONAL WILDLIFE REFUGE

Description: One of the newest refuges within the National Wildlife Refuge System, the Cape May NWR will eventually protect 17,000 acres of critically important habitat. The area includes forest, marshes, and fields. The Delaware Bay shoreline is one of the major spring shorebird staging areas in North America.

Viewing Information: The best wildlife viewing opportunities are in spring and fall. During fall migration, American woodcock concentrate on the Cape May Peninsula. Fall migration also brings large numbers of raptors. The birds pause on the peninsula to feed and rest before crossing the open water of Delaware Bay. In fall, motorists can view hawks directly from roads that run perpendicular to the beaches and New Jersey 47. Since the refuge is new, few public use facilities are in place. Existing foot trails provide excellent birding opportunities. Trails are accessible from Bobwhite and Woodcock lanes off NJ 47, south of Kimbles Beach Road. Vehicles are prohibited on trails.

Directions: *From New Jersey 9 in Cape May Court House, take County Route 658 west to New Jersey 47. Turn left (south) onto NJ 47 and then right onto Kimbles Beach Road. The office is on your right.*

Ownership: U.S. Fish and Wildlife Service (609) 463-0994

Size: Approximately 8,000 acres   **Closest Town:** Cape May Court House

Cape May NWR provides critical habitat for American woodcock, which concentrate on the Cape May Peninsula during fall migration. The birds will remain in the area into December as long as the ground remains unfrozen.
CLAY MYERS

The shorebird viewing areas have easy access to bayshore beaches. Visit one or more of these sites in May to witness something amazing: thousands of horseshoe crabs arriving on the beaches of Delaware Bay for spawning. Millions of their small green eggs are laid in the sand and become food for birds. Red knots, ruddy turnstones, semipalmated sandpipers, laughing gulls, dunlins, sanderlings, and least sandpipers arrive by the thousands to feast on the eggs. For migrating shorebirds, this stop is essential to provide the food they need to continue on to their Arctic nesting grounds.

NORBURYS LANDING

Description: Norburys Landing is a small, sand parking area and turn-around with an observation area for a view of the beach along Delaware Bay.

Viewing Information: Do not walk on the beach during the shorebird migration period in May, simply scan the beach and the bay from the parking area or the viewing platform. At other times of the year, look north toward Reeds Beach. The creek that empties into the bay is a favorite feeding spot for gulls, herons, and egrets.

Directions: *From Garden State Parkway exit 4, take New Jersey 47 west and north for 3.2 miles. Turn left on Norburys Landing Road at the sign for the Villas. Continue straight to Norburys Landing when main road bends to the left and becomes Bay Shore Road.*

Ownership: Middle Township (609) 628-2436   **Closest Town:** Villas

Eighty percent of the East's red knots congregate on Delaware Bay beaches each spring to feast on eggs laid by breeding horseshoe crabs. The spectacle draws viewers from around the world. CLAY MYERS

REEDS BEACH

Description: The northern end of the small town of Reeds Beach has remnant sand dunes and coastal vegetation. In May, an observation platform is erected on the beach for shorebird viewing by NJDFGW/ENSP staff. From the end of the road and the privately owned parking lot, there is an excellent view of a salt marsh. OPEN MAY 1–JUNE 10.

Viewing Information: Look at Reeds Beach from the observation deck or the jetty at the end of the road. Do not walk on the beaches during the spring shorebird migration. Disturbance cause the birds to stop feeding, which may mean the difference between life and death for them.

Directions: *Reeds Beach Road is slightly more than 2 miles north of Norburys Landing Road on New Jersey 47. Turn left and travel 1 mile into town. Turn right onto Beach Avenue and continue to parking lot at the end of the road.*

DO NOT PARK ON THE SIDES OF THE ROAD IN THE TOWN.

Ownership: Multiple owners; call (609) 628-2436 for information

Closest Town: Reeds Beach

FORTESCUE GLADES

Description: The Natural Lands Trust is undertaking a dune restoration project in the fishing resort of Fortescue, just south of the public beach. This portion of the Glades, as the extensive holding of land is known, is adjacent to the salt marsh of Egg Island Wildlife Management Area.

Viewing Information: Park on the side of the road past the beach bulkhead, where the dunes begin (look for Natural Lands Trust signs). Walk south toward the creek that bisects the beach and flows into the bay. Cross over the dunes only at specified locations. Do not walk on the beach or along the creek when migrating shorebirds are feeding.

Directions: *From County Route 553 in Cedarville, go south for 2 miles to County Route 629. Turn right and travel 0.8 mile to Baptist Road. Turn right on Baptist Road, travel 0.3 mile to Fortescue Road, and turn left. Proceed for 4 miles to the town of Fortescue. As you cross the bridge into town, Fortescue Road becomes Downe Avenue. Proceed for 0.4 mile to a T intersection. Turn left and travel 1.1 miles to the end of the bulkhead. Park on the edge of the road.*

Ownership: Natural Lands Trust (610) 353-5587

Closest Town: Fortescue

Description: Lying adjacent to the coastal forest section of Belleplain State Forest is one of the finest salt marshes in the state. The upland edge of the marsh has some of the best birding along the coast of Delaware Bay. The tidal creeks, abundant with white perch and blue crabs, are an essential nursery for many species of fish and shellfish.

Viewing Information: Stop frequently along Jake's Landing Road in the spring to look and listen for the spring songbird migrants. The vistas of the marsh as you leave the forest are guaranteed to take your breath away. As you enjoy the scenery, keep your eyes open for northern harriers and short-eared owls hunting over the marsh. Harriers are sometimes spotted perching on a mat of grass, but more frequently their diagnostic white rumps are observed while they are in flight. Stay until dusk to see the short-eared owls dancing like butterflies over the marsh. Rails are more frequently heard than seen in the spring, summer, and fall. Listen for the distinctive "kek-kek-kek-kek" of the clapper rail in particular. Waterfowl include occasional northern pintails, American wigeons, abundant American black ducks, mallards, and frequent mergansers.

Dennis Creek WMA is a natural area with no facilities.

OPEN FOR HUNTING DURING PRESCRIBED SEASONS.

Directions: *From the intersection of New Jersey 47 and County Route 557 in Dennis Township, travel 0.3 mile south to Jake's Landing Road. Turn right and proceed 1.5 miles to the parking lot, boat ramp, and Dennis Creek.*

Ownership: NJDEP, Division of Fish, Game, and Wildlife (609) 629-0090

Size: 5,414 acres   **Closest Towns:** North Dennis and Dennisville

Unlike most other fish-eating herons, the yellow-crowned night heron eats mostly fiddler crabs, mussels, and snails in coastal marshes. A. AND E. MORRIS

Description: The varied habitats of this WMA include river and tidal marsh boundary, freshwater impoundments, diked hay meadows, and oak-pine uplands. The Maurice River, designated Wild and Scenic, flows past the area to the Delaware Bay. East Point Lighthouse, an old, scenic structure still in service, is maintained by the Maurice River Historical Society. It is located at the southern end of the WMA. A driving tour of the area includes a route around the impoundments, past the tidal marsh, and through the woods on sand roads. For your own comfort, avoid the biting-fly season in mid-summer.

Viewing Information: Birders visit Heislerville WMA to see thousands of wintering snow geese and the occasional bald eagle. Northern pintails, buffleheads, red-breasted mergansers, canvasbacks, and green-winged teal also spend the winter here. Mute swans live here year-round. In the spring and fall, the tidal mud flats are filled with migrating shorebirds. Horseshoe crabs spawn on nearby Moores Beach and East Point in May. The horseshoe crab eggs provide protein-rich food for red knots, ruddy turnstones, and semi-palmated sandpipers that stop here as they travel to their Arctic breeding grounds. Rental boats and boat ramps are available along the Maurice River.

Heislerville WMA is a natural area with no facilities. EXERCISE CAUTION WHEN DRIVING ON SANDY ROADS. OPEN FOR HUNTING DURING PRESCRIBED SEASONS.

Directions: *From the southern end of New Jersey 55 and its intersection with New Jersey 47, travel 5.3 miles on NJ 47 south to Mackey's Lane. Turn right onto Mackey's Lane and proceed 0.3 mile to County Route 616 (Dorchester–Heislerville Road). Turn left and travel 2.2 miles to Matts Landing Road. Turn right and proceed 1 mile past the impoundments to a parking area on left.*

Ownership: NJDEP, Division of Fish, Game, and Wildlife (609) 292-9450

Size: 4,876 acres   **Closest Town:** Heislerville, Maurice River Township

The green heron is a shy bird, often skulking away among the grass along the water's edge at the first sign of an intruder. Look for them along shorelines or muddy flats at low tide. HARRY W. KOCH

CAPE MAY / DELAWARE BAY

80. MORIE SAND COMPANY

Description: North Pond Park includes a 49-acre pond, a 30-acre sand and mud flat, a wildflower meadow, butterfly garden, and a walking trail up to the woodland areas.

Viewing Information: The forest edges provide excellent habitat for white-tailed deer and red foxes. The trail affords the hiker several good views of the pond. Look for waterfowl in the fall and winter. Osprey and bald eagles nest in the area, and are seen frequently in the park.

Directions: *From the southern end of New Jersey 55 and its intersection with New Jersey 47, continue almost 3 miles to a traffic light. Turn right (west) toward Mauricetown and Port Norris and proceed 2.2 miles to Noble Street (2nd blinking light). Turn left and go 0.8 mile to the plant on the right and parking lot on the left.*

Ownership: The Morie Company, Inc. Mauricetown Division (609) 785-0720

Size: North Pond Park, 135 acres   **Closest Town:** Mauricetown

81. EGG ISLAND WILDLIFE MANAGEMENT AREA

Description: This WMA is a vast, windswept salt marsh, dotted with hummocks of cedar trees, bayberry bushes, sumac, and common reeds. Numerous tidal creeks await the explorer, crabber, or angler. There is a large pond in the middle of the tract, accessible only by boat, that wintering waterfowl find attractive. The Glades, a large tract of open space protected by Natural Lands Trust, borders the WMA.

Viewing Information: Park in the small area at the end of the road and take the footbridge into the WMA. Walk any of the trails into the marsh. Look for mussels and fiddler crabs at the edge of the water, and egrets and herons in the marsh. Northern harriers and many species of gulls can be seen. Thousands of snow geese frequent the marsh in winter. For your own comfort, avoid the biting-fly season in midsummer. Egg Island WMA is a natural area with no facilities. OPEN FOR HUNTING DURING PRESCRIBED SEASONS.

Directions: *From the southern end of New Jersey 55 where it intersects with New Jersey 47, continue south on NJ 47 for 3.2 miles to the traffic light. Turn right (west) toward Mauricetown and Port Norris. Travel 2.2 miles to Highland Street (2nd blinking light). Turn right and proceed 5.3 miles (Highland Street becomes County Route 676) to a T intersection with County Route 553. Turn right onto CR 553 and proceed 0.2 mile to Maple Street on your left. Take Maple Street 2.7 miles to the end of the road and the footbridge onto the WMA.*

Ownership: NJDEP, Division of Fish, Game, and Wildlife (609) 629-0090

Size: 6,714 acres   **Closest Town:** Fortescue

82. BAYSIDE

Description: This extensive coastal wetlands tract along the Delaware Bay has tidal creeks, woods, and grasslands for a variety of wildlife. Remnants of the town known as Caviar, named for the historic export of sturgeon caviar, are visible in the water and marsh along the bay. Traces of railroad tracks can still be seen at low tide near the observation deck.

Viewing Information: Spring and fall migrations bring waterfowl, shorebirds, songbirds, and hawks for birders to pursue with binoculars. Late spring and early summer, before the biting-fly season, offer outstanding birding in nearby cultivated fields and salt marshes. Ring-billed gulls flock to the fields for feeding. Marsh wrens and willets sing and call loudly throughout the nesting season. Look for them on the edges of the salt marsh. Listen for the distinctive *"kek-kek-kek-kek"* of the clapper rail. American black ducks nest near the creeks in the marsh grasses. Muskrat lodges dot the landscape of the marsh, while fiddler crabs and mussels are visible in the creeks at low tide.

Directions: *From the junction of New Jersey 49 and New Jersey 77 in Bridgeton, proceed 0.7 mile west on NJ 49 to left turn onto West Avenue. Proceed 0.2 mile to right turn on County Route 607. Continue for 6.9 miles to the center of Greenwich. Turn right on County Route 623, then left on County Route 642. Continue on CR 642 for 1.7 miles to a T intersection. Turn right to Bayside and continue for 0.3 mile to an unmarked left turn onto a sand road. Follow the sand road for 1.7 miles to the observation deck on the bay.*

Ownership: Public Service Electric and Gas (PSE&G) (609)339-7915

Size: About 4,500 acres   **Closest Town:** Greenwich

The oystercatcher's bill is long and compressed, like an oysterman's knife, allowing it to poke into the half-opened shells of bivalves and pry them open. As its name implies, it eats oysters, as well as clams, crabs, and marine worms.
A. AND E. MORRIS

83. BRIDGETON CITY PARK

Description: Bridgeton City Park, established in 1898, sits in the middle of the bustling county seat of Cumberland County. The park has two lakes and a pond, connected by a waterway known as the Raceway. A concessionaire offers canoe rentals on the Raceway and Sunset Lake. Cohanzick Zoo, Nail House Museum, and a Swedish Farmstead Museum are other attractions. Between the zoo and Cohansey River, east of the park, there is a coastal area holly forest.

Viewing Information: Fishing is a popular pastime at the City Park. Bald eagles fish at Sunset Lake in the winter, great blue herons are seen in the spring and summer, and river otters ply the Raceway and Cohansey River year-round. Park near the zoo for trails that parallel the Raceway east toward the Cohansey River. Look for muskrats and wetlands birds in the marshes near the river's edge. The sand roads and trails around Mary Elmer Lake and Sunset Lake are in an upland pine-oak forest. It is good habitat for Fowler's toads, hognose snakes, southern leopard frogs, and eastern box turtles. Fall and spring migration provide great birding.

Directions: *From the intersection of New Jersey 49 and New Jersey 77 in Bridgeton, go west on NJ 49 for 0.2 mile to Atlantic Street. Turn right and travel 1 long block to the park entrance straight ahead. Atlantic Street becomes Mayor Aitken Drive as you enter the park. Continue on Aitken Drive, paralleling the Raceway, for approximately 0.5 mile. Parking is available at the lot near the zoo (on right). At Park Drive, turn left (west). In 0.5 mile turn right onto West Avenue. Access to Sunset Lake's roads and trails is on your right.*

Ownership: City of Bridgeton (609) 455-3230

Size: About 1100 acres   **Closest Town:** Bridgeton

One of the neotropical songbirds, the northern oriole breeds in temperate woodlands and winters in the tropics. TOM VEZO

FOWSER ROAD PARK MUNICIPAL BOAT RAMP

Description: The boat ramp in Millville is one of the few access points along the nationally designated Wild and Scenic Maurice River and its tributaries (the Menantico and Manumuskin rivers and Muskee Creek). The diversity of natural communities in these watersheds make them a haven of biodiversity. Large tracts of undeveloped swamp forest and pine and oak upland forest are found along the river's banks, and tidal marshes surround the Maurice's confluence with the Delaware Bay. Rentals are not available at the site; bring your own boat. No fishing or swimming is allowed from the pier. Motor boats should stay in the main channel of the Maurice River, since there are dangerous obstructions in the tributaries and marsh channels, and strandings are likely at low tides.

Viewing Information: More than 40 miles of waterway within the Wild and Scenic study area give you many opportunities for viewing wildlife. Of particular importance are the wild rice marshes, one of the last remaining stands in New Jersey. Wild rice is an important food for ducks and rails. Bald eagles and northern harriers stay year-round. Belted kingfishers are frequently seen from the boat ramp pier. In the spring and summer the river comes alive with the herring run. Look for nesting ospreys, bank swallows, Forster's terns, and least terns. Muskrat lodges built of sticks and reeds are visible in the marshes. For your own comfort, avoid the biting-fly season in midsummer. Just to the south of the boat ramp, the first large wild rice marsh to the east is part of the Peek Preserve, owned by Natural Lands Trust, Inc., which manages the 252-acre property as a wildlife refuge. Access to the preserve is open by appointment to school groups and interested conservationists by calling (610) 353-5587 at least one week in advance.

Directions: *From the intersection of New Jersey 47 and New Jersey 49 in Millville, go south on NJ 47 for 1 mile. Turn right (west) on Fowser Road. Parking for cars and boat trailers is available at the boat ramp site.*

Ownership: City of Millville (609) 825-7000

Closest Town: Millville

The Maurice River system supports some of the most important and rare wildlife habitats in the Cape May–Delaware Bay region. Research indicates that more than half of New Jersey's threatened and endangered plants and animals reside in the 380-square-mile watershed.

Description: One of the largest wildlife management areas in the state, Peaslee has thousands of acres of upland pine-oak forests and lowland bogs. Its longest border is the upper part of the Tuckahoe River. Old cranberry bogs and a mill area offer excellent freshwater marsh habitats.

Viewing Information: Take the loop road for views of a variety of habitats. The sand road takes you past a wooded edge, typical pinelands, cedar bog and hardwood swamp, scrub oak forest, sweet ferns and field, and finally, managed plantings of yellow clover pasture and grassy fields. Look for Allegheny ant mounds, white-tailed deer, wild turkeys, northern water snakes, prairie warblers, and bobwhite quail.

Peaslee WMA is a natural area with no facilities. EXERCISE CAUTION WHEN DRIVING ON SANDY ROADS. OPEN FOR HUNTING DURING PRESCRIBED SEASONS.

Directions: *From New Jersey 55 exit 24, take New Jersey 49 east to Hesstown Road, about 5 miles. Turn left and proceed 1.7 miles to the sand road on your left. Turn left on the sand road for a 1.6 mile auto tour loop. You will exit at Hesstown Road. To get to Bennetts Mill, return on Hesstown Road to NJ 49. Turn right (west) and travel 1.2 miles to County Route 671 (Union Road). Turn right and travel 4 miles to Old Mays Landing Road (first right turn). Turn right and travel less than 1 mile to bridge. Mill pond is on your left.*

Ownership: NJDEP, Division of Fish, Game, and Wildlife (609) 629-0090

Size: 19,923 acres   **Closest Town:** Millville

Tiger salamanders are members of the mole salamander family, which refers to their burrowing ability and desire to spend most of the time underground. Increasingly rare in New Jersey, these salamanders emerge from their winter burrows and migrate to ice-covered breeding ponds in midwinter. ROBERT T. ZAPPALORTI

86. OCEAN CITY VIEWING AREAS

Description: Ocean City is a popular shore destination for families in the summer. See some of the nearby bird families from the 12th Street Pavilion in the middle of town. The pavilion overlooks Great Egg Harbor Bay for a great view of Cowpens Island Wildlife Sanctuary (off limits to visitors). Cowpens Island is one of the few places on the southern New Jersey coast where large numbers of migratory wading birds nest. An abandoned railroad right-of-way at the south end of the city offers pedestrians a chance to see birds out feeding.

Viewing Information: Opportunities vary with the season, but exist year-round. In summer, from the pavilion, look for herons and ibises leaving Cowpens Island at dawn and returning to their nests at dusk. Walking on the railroad bed from town takes you out to the Intracoastal Waterway through the salt marsh. There are excellent opportunities here for seeing herons, egrets, terns, osprey, and black skimmers. Muskrats and river otters live in the marsh.

Directions: From Garden State Parkway exit 25, take County Route 623 east 1 mile to Ocean City. Turn right (south) on West Avenue and proceed 2 miles to 51st Street. Turn right and take 51st Street to Haven Avenue. Access to the railroad bed is straight ahead. Park along Haven Avenue. To get to the pavilion from CR 623, turn left onto Bay Avenue and proceed to 12th Street. Turn left (west) and proceed to the bay. The pavilion is straight ahead. Park on the street.

Ownership: City of Ocean City (609) 525-9335

Size: Pavilion is 1600 square feet   **Closest Town:** Ocean City

87. WETLANDS INSTITUTE

Description: From the lecture hall inside the Wetlands Institute, 6,000 acres of pristine salt marsh are visible. Shore traffic is intense in July and August, so plan on delays and be careful on the highway. The institute sponsors a large "Wings 'n Water" festival in September. Other programs are available.

Viewing Information: The Wetlands Institute has a delightful education center with hands-on exhibits for youngsters. Climb the tower for a bird's-eye view of New Jersey's coastal landscape, stand on the large observation deck to savor the unique salt marsh smells, or walk the 0.25-mile nature trail through the salt marsh to a wide creek. Northern diamondback terrapins are North America's only salt marsh turtle. During egg-laying season, June and July, they frequently cross the roads. Be careful!

Directions: Take Exit 10 from the Garden State Parkway, east toward Stone Harbor. The institute is 2.9 miles, on the right side of the road.

Ownership: Private (609) 368-1211

Size: 34 acres   **Closest Town:** Stone Harbor

WILDLIFE INDEX

Discover the Thrill of Watching Wildlife.